ENERGY HEALING & SOUL MEDICINE

CURATED BY RADHAA NILIA

RADHAA
PUBLISHING HOUSE

DEDICATION

*For everyone who wishes to heal themselves, others,
and our world!*

~

FOREWORD

My name is Raziel Arcega, and I have been blessed to know Radhaa Nilia as the curator of "Energy Healing & Soul Medicine" book. I have known Radhaa for over a decade as she's always been into the healing arts. Over time, she's become a dear friend and ally in my life, both professionally and personally. I never thought (in a million years) I'd be a published author myself. But through the inspiration and support I have received from Radhaa, I was able to pursue my writing dreams that surpassed anything I could ever imagine.

I became a co-author in the best-selling book series "Awakening Starseeds." I've also been a contributing writer to "Pillars of Light: Goddess Activations" and the forthcoming book "Infinite Cosmic Records: Sacred Doorways to Healing & Remembering"—by Radhaa Publishing House. These opportunities came because I had done my inner healing work. Energy Healing has given me the Courage, Vision, and Strength to pursue my deepest desires. I was able to clear fears of visibility and vulnerability to transcend these limitations into my superpower.

And now, it is my honor to write this foreword for the Energy Healing & Soul Medicine book, knowing I have been a recipient of many healing methods over the years. Experiencing these modalities provided profound shifts in my life and has positively impacted my children's lives. *"My children can see their own mother pursuing her passions and being brave, giving them confidence that they can do the same."*

I am grateful and relieved to know all types of modalities and healers are available right here, right now. It excites me to know that I can open pages of this book and feel I can connect to just about any healer of my choice. Having the opportunity to experience a variety of Masterful healers in this book makes it easier for me to think positively in my healing journey in upgrading my well-being. It inspired me to step into my own healing career—Nutrition practitioner and consultant.

We don't have to carry the pain of our lineage, circumstances, and our limiting beliefs. We can replace old, and outdated beliefs. I encourage anyone ready for a positive shift in their life to read this book and get to know the type of healer or coach you feel called to connect with. Because investing in your physical, mental, emotional, and spiritual well-being is one of the most valuable investments you can ever make. I am excited for you to pick this book up and learn the many modalities and methods. As we heal, we create Peace of mind available for us and others to experience. Miracles await!

Blessings on your Healing Journey!

- Raziel Arcega

From the Desk of a Humanitarian Filmmaker Activist:

*"**Energy** comes from the Greek word, '**Energeia**,' which means: Action, Activity, and Operation. Healing comes from the old English that means 'restoration to health.' And "Soul" is from the Proto-Germanic: Saiwalo--the Source. With this book, Energy Healing & Soul Medicine, will trigger the medicine within you that will, indeed, restore you to the true self, to the Source of your being, allowing you to complete the sentence: 'I think therefore I am...therefore I do.' The new shift, the new XXIst century Ré-évolution is the revolution of the soul, the Source. This is how we tap into our essence, to our Spirit. Spirit comes from the Latin word 'Espiritu,' which means 'Breath.' Breath in and breath out each word from this inspiring book. In oneness, we shall heal ourselves, heal each other, and heal the World. You will wake up, whole again, and you will be on propulsion towards the path to the true meaning, true action in your life. More than ever, I invite you to embrace this book. Radhaa Nilia's glorious creation is a tool of atomic awakening to finally establish a viable future made of pure Peace and of pure Love. Highly recommended book!" Namaste.*

Emmanuel Itier
Humanitarian, Filmmaker and Political Activist
Www.Wonderlandentgroup.com

INTRODUCTION

In a time filled with uncertainty, it seems like we are calling for help from all places where people of such strength in mind, heart, and soul can offer humanity support in these most challenging times in our lives. Therefore, we bring you various healing modalities to assist you and connect with what feels aligned with your needs.

This book gathers high-caliber healers and coaches who share their heartfelt stories, wisdom, and introduction to various modalities. With this, we humbly offer you gifts of healing. Take full advantage of the authentic healers and coaches in this book. Get to know them and be inspired by the stories they bring to share with you how they overcame their struggles to realize their most potent connection with the Divine — a source of healing power.

May you find the positive light in the next pages to keep your health and well-being at your best, and be comforted knowing there are many healing tools available to empower your journey and life.

Do not hesitate to connect with these incredible healers, mystics, coaches, and conduits of transformation. We are here to support and lift us together towards the doorway from darkness to light. We send you infinite healing, love, and light!

— Radhaa Publishing House

CONTENTS

1. INFINITE COSMIC RECORDS   1
Maya Verzonilla, AKA Maya The Shaman   11

2. THE ASSIGNMENT   13
Lori Thayer, Ph.D.   23

3. BUTTERFLY HEALING   25
Patricia Wald-Hopkins   35

4. UNSTOPPABLE HEALING   37
Leslie Allyn Finkel   47

5. ANGEL   49
Amanda Waterman   57

6. FINDING MY SUPERPOWER   59
Misty Pennington   69

7. HEALING ANCESTRAL LINEAGE   71
Meredith Ruben Daniels   79

8. EVOLUTION OF CONSCIOUSNESS   81
Neil Gaur   87

9. MADE OF STARDUST   89
Eva Vennari   99

10. FALLING IN LOVE WITH DEATH   101
Eric Raines   107

11. 40 LAYERS OF THE AURA   109
Annemiek Douw MSc   119

12. I AM THE UNIVERSE   121
Brittany Marie Fouche, AKA Marie Universe   129

13. WHEN A PILOT FALLS DOWN   131
Amy Thain Jorgensen   139

14. HEAVEN ON EARTH WITH ASHTAR   141
Lalitah Sunra   149

15. SACRED RELATIONSHIP ALCHEMY   151
Stasia Bliss   159

16. IN THIS WORLD, NOT OF IT   161
Lezlie Mitchell (B.Msc, B.A. English)   167

17. TRANQUIL COMPANION   169
   Maureen Keller   175
18. SPINNING GODDESS HEALER   177
   Danielle Schreck   183
19. GODDESS ACTIVATIONS™   185

   Radhaa Nilia   197
   ABOUT RADHAA PUBLISHING HOUSE   199

1

INFINITE COSMIC RECORDS
BY: MAYA THE SHAMAN

Courage To Be a Seeker

My mystical experience with "Infinite Cosmic Records" came to me through the grace of two Spiritual Masters from the East, from my Lemurian Shamanic lineage, my great-great-Grandfather, Don Pedro, and an ascended Master from India, Shrii Shrii Anandamurtiji.

The Clarion Call

I believe that the 3D realm is a fragile-volatile dimension and must be guarded by light warriors to safeguard our precious life on Earth. In this understanding, I aspire, when the day will come that the worst part of history is just a dream of the past, where a bright future and shift of consciousness will take the stage front and center.

In this mass awakening, I hear the Clarion Call — envisioning standing for humanity's wellbeing to remember our birthright, claim our Freedom, Sovereignty, Peace, and Happiness.

Time of Change is Upon Us

The story of human civilization has many ups and downs. History has been a battlefield of physical, mental, emotional, and spiritual realms. A cycle is repeating itself, yet this time, another opportunity awaits for humanity to correct the old template of crime against humanity — 26 thousand years of waiting in darkness, from Kali Yuga (dark ages), we are moving towards Satya Yuga (age of light and truth).

Though many are afraid, and others don't even know how to deal with certain traumatic issues in our world, the most relevant and profound information for anyone to know is that YOU have the answers. You came here for a reason – you choose to live and witness this transition from darkness to light!

We are in between these two cycles, and the dark age is smacked with the age of light for us to experience. So, hold steady because this movement towards the age of truth seeks light warriors to be the seers, affirming for a bright future, and take the courage to strengthen the human spirit as we cross the bridge to the other side in our physical bodies towards the Golden Age. Let the relative truth pass, for the eternal truth remains. There's a beautiful saying by a spiritual Master, Anandamurtiji.

"The future is brighter than you can ever imagine."
~ Shrii Shrii Anandamurtiji.

We have reached a plateau in the playing field between dark realm and light, now is the real deal – a time to trust the

Supreme Creator of all that is, the supreme source of all creation in this Universe and multiverse that we are being carried into this new — age of light, despite the discombobulated realities being thrown into our realm. We needed to refocus our vision, hold the light, and never let it go.

The Grand Cosmic Test

This cycle of transition is the grand Cosmic test. Learning the difference between attachment and detachment to negative or positive energies is essential now more than ever to recognize. Seek Discernment.

To realize your job is to prioritize your self-healing, self-understanding of consciousness creates more direct control over your thoughts, mind, and spirit in this worldly game humans play.

Moving inwards into our spirit, we access the unconditional love living deep within us. According to an enlightened Master, Anandamurtiji, universal love is the answer to our broken world. We are to recreate a new world — a new Earth, through our love connection with the Divine. It is the meaning of spirituality. And this is what I have personally experienced.

I am about to share a tragedy that turned into the most inspiring moment of my existence on Earth and has found Supreme consciousness at work.

Glimpse into my Story

My Father worked as an engineer in a Greek ship when he encountered a thunderous stormy night with giant tidal waves while crossing the Red China sea. No one can escape this tragedy. It was inevitable, karmic in nature, and has already been predestined by fate. My Father was our sole provider, and with it, my entire family depended on him. We mourned for his loss, terrified for who would take care of us then. He sacrificed his Life for his family; fed, clothed, housed, and schooled us — our lives were in his hands. Lost at sea, Father left behind a traumatized family, not knowing what the future holds. He's gone!

This incident occurred in Maharlika (the Philippines) when I was seventeen. Maharlika, being its original name, was once a part of Lemuria — the largest continent of the Pacific that sank in the ocean long ago. Stories about the land and its original people cloaked in unspoken mystery. The mystical part of it came to me during the most traumatic time in my Life – lost at sea father.

Amid our mourning of losing my Father, a friend visited me and taught me how to meditate. She said it would assist me out of the deep sadness and depression if I did my Yoga and meditations daily. I have no other alternative but to follow her advice because, for 17 years old me, I needed guidance. In my traumatic condition, I moved inwards. I focused on my breath in and out, becoming aware of the Life flowing through me. I hold unto it with all my intention to replace illusive ungrounded thoughts bothering me.

Sacred Mantras - Love and Light

I did not know this when I began my practice. I was trying to calm down my wrecked teenager nerves from the tragedy my entire family had experienced. But little do I know what would happen next. As I got deeper into my spiritual practice, I chanted, fasted, became a complete vegetarian, meditated, and followed the 16 points code of ethics and rituals that comes as an avid Yoga practitioner.

I fixed my gaze at my altar daily, reminding me of the spiritual duties I perform every day. I did not know what else to do in my teens since my Mother cried a lot, my brother drowned himself in alcohol, my sister lost herself with friends, and I was focused on my newly found practice. Each of us has our separate ways of dealing with our stress. As I continued to practice my meditations daily and kept increasing my sitting time in lotus posture from 2 to 4 hours each time, I was glued.

Living Light and Love Mantra – "Baba Nam Kevalam"

I radically increased my meditations to four times a day, sitting long hours. Surprisingly, that was all I wanted to do at that time! I discovered this Mantra was a "living light-love technology for the spirit." The mantra 'Baba Nam Kevalam' I practiced grew inside of me. The more I meditated and chanted with it, its power increased. When I temporarily stopped, I noticed that it would repeat itself back to me like a boomerang! I found love with the Mantra, feeling I could not live without it. Then one night, something mysterious happened.

Discovery of Infinite Cosmic Records

I went to bed, half asleep and half awake. Suddenly, I have spun around by force greater than my own. Swirling so fast, moving out of this planet into a vast space passing through stars, planets, and galaxies — *so vast, it feels infinite* —I was carried away at the speed of light! It repeated for seven consecutive nights of cosmic travel without sleep, fully awake, in a trance-like realm. I have no control of this reality. Yet, it felt blissful, and I felt safe, at home. I realized that I was granted a key to the Cosmic portal to this glorious Universe. Realizing my DNA contains the micro template of the infinite macro Universe that mirrored the Divine Cosmos was Epic!

"I realized my micro Universe resides within my 'I am presence' wrapped-up in a skin suit."

What a discovery!

Graced with a Cosmic boon, I continued to move further inwards and meditated a whole lot more. Nothing seemed to matter anymore in my perspective of the world. The most appropriate companion after my Father's Death was silence, and with my new internal compass, I did not speak for a year. Navigating towards deeper union with the sacred, I found a magical realm — out of this world.

Born under the sign of Cancer, I am naturally psychic. My 3rd eye chakra opened, and I could see my future clearly in front of me. Still, I even got a heightened sensitivity when my crown chakra's antennas picked up all types of relevant information, reading what's underneath the surface. My senses became so subtle that I could hear peoples' thoughts even when others around me were not speaking, and No, I was not crazy! I can send messages telepathically to loved ones and receive their message too.

As my spiritual practice further awakened my 6th sense, I became fearless. I even followed the Tantric path. 'To release and confront darkness, I meditated in the graveyard, all night long to face my deepest fears!'

Shortly, everything started to shift. I become consciously hyper-aware. I can step out of my body into the ethers, in and out of my body. In my meditations, instantly, I would astral project, looking down at myself 5-7 feet above my body. Laid in my bed, I'm on the ceiling, looking down at me. When I visit a place that does not resonate with my energy, I move upwards in space, flying. Time and space become irrelevant. Other times, I get to see other souls in the astral realm. I felt self-contained and safe. It was the beginning of knowing my connection with the Divine.

In the meantime, my Mother used all her skills to immigrate to the USA after my Father's Death to provide a better future for my siblings and me. The US immigration doctor in the Philippines halted my departure when he found I had tuberculosis. I was not allowed to enter the country. Miraculously, on my return to the Doctor for the next X-ray exam, he was stunned and couldn't believe what had happened. My final X-ray test was clear and free – within two weeks, my lungs showed no signs of damage, but perfect. Both X-rays were placed side by side, and the Doctor, who was in disbelief, had no alternative but to sign my immigration papers of release for my travels. It was how I came to America and immigrated with my mother and siblings. I believed that my spiritual practice produced the desired outcome. This incident is just one of the multiple miraculous experiences I've had.

Shamanism – My Indigenous Lemurian Lineage Link

After my ascended Master Anandamurtiji left his body, my Lemurian Shaman great-great-Grandfather's energy appeared. Shamanism aligned to my Tantra Yoga path back to my Lemurian ancestry. (The Tantra Yoga I practiced has nothing to do with the famous Western Tantra Sex - the inverted Tantra.) Authentic Tantra Yoga embraces deep wisdom and devotion through meditation and self-realization, which is highly revered and sacred in the East.

My great-great-Grandfather Shaman, Don Pedro

Don Pedro is a Lemurian Galactic-portal-timekeeper Shaman. Every Shaman is unique, and Don Pedro is certainly one. He would knock through walls to let me know he was around. Then information comes through visions and channeled messages, and he showed me my past life incarnation as a Native Cherokee American Indian through many visions that came through me.

In Human Design, I have been classified as a 'time traveler—foresight seer.' Just like my great-great-Grandfather Shaman, Don Pedro's genetic coding, opening doorways to Cosmic portals — I have inherited his Maharlikan-Lemurian shamanic way.

In retrospect, Don Pedro supported many visions related to places and people connected to my past incarnations. Don Pedro guided me also to meet Isa, daughter of a Maharlikan Shaman portal keeper of the Lemurian Crystals kingdom beneath the pacific ocean.

The Courage to Remember

In summary, I see the wave of awakening is coming to Earth for a great remembrance as part of this Infinite Cosmic realm, not separate, but as builders of life force to be protected while living in this challenging and limited 3D realm awaiting the next phase of our human destiny to experience our galactic connection.

Life is sacred. Those who destroy precious lives on Earth have a heavy karmic paying to do, for the force guiding the stars and this Universe is awake and contains all actions and deeds written on the Cosmic Records. 'All human history and cosmic history are in the safekeeping of the Great mysterious Records of All There Is.'

What is Infinite Cosmic Records?

"INFINITE COSMIC RECORDS" is a benevolent, sacred, safe healing method. A Tantric-Shamanic-Cosmic method where my clients journey with me to retrieve their forgotten past lives to understand their present and future. By peeling off many layers of the self, whom you think you are in the moment, you'll discover you're more than you think! More of you are hidden beneath layers of coverings, and your true self emerges in this journey. Your Cosmic Records are stored in the safekeeping of this Universe, where nothing is ever lost.

Infinite Cosmic Records & Lemurian Code Healing Modalities

Infinite Cosmic Records became the foundation of my spiritual journey and healing methods. My original healing modality, **Lemurian Code Healing**, supported my method of **Infinite Cosmic Records** through the sacred doorways to Healing and Remembering—*"Who am I and Why am I here?"* While Tantra Yoga led me to the Infinite Cosmic Realm, and Lemurian Shamanism brought me the awareness of many past lives I've had.

Humans have always asked: Is there more to this Life? When a spiritual ascended Master, Anandamurtiji says, *"The future is brighter than you can ever imagine."* He also said he is an *"eternal optimist,"* and I believe it. The Creator of this great Universe has a Cosmic plan. As co-creators, together, we can create a bright future.

I invite you to dive deep into your cosmic records with me. The Infinite Cosmic Records are available for you to experience massive healing. As a sincere, true seeker, you will be given the pathway to your cosmic records. Clients arrived at our session wanting to be their very own seers, to look into their Cosmic Records during their sessions, and while I guide them in this journey, I see what they see, I feel what they feel, and when lost, I take them back and keep them safe. It's the kind that expands your consciousness and fills you up until you remember who you are.

Today, I share the infinite cosmic records method with my clients, and they too--get to experience their Cosmic Records through their sessions with me. In my forthcoming stand-alone book, coming Summer 2022, the*"Infinite Cosmic Records: Sacred Doorways to Healing & Remembering,"* you can read stories shared by my clients to inspire you.

Welcome to your Infinite Cosmic Records, dear Ones!

"Allow me to be your Shaman guide to the Cosmic Discovery of your Records. Awaken your past to understand your present and future realm."

Thank you — Salamat Po,
~Maya The Shaman

∾

MAYA VERZONILLA, AKA MAYA THE SHAMAN

ABOUT THE AUTHOR

Maya The Shaman, is a Shaman Healer, Life and Writing Coach, and the Creatrix of original healing modalities, "Lemurian Code Healing" & "Infinite Cosmic Records."

She is a Co-Author of the collaborative book series "Awakening Starseeds" and contributing writer to "Pillars of Light." Her stand-alone forthcoming books are "Infinite Cosmic

Records: Sacred Doorways to Healing and Remembering," Summer 2022, and "Descendants of Lemuria," coming by 2023.

She appeared in several documentary films, "The Cure" by Hollywood's French Director Emmanuel Itier, Produced by Actress Sharon Stone, where visions, wisdom, and inspiration are infused to achieve planetary transformation. Another documentary film Maya was invited was "Guns, Bombs, War: A love story," where war cries cannot be ignored as 'wars are crimes against humanity!'

To get a *FREE Consultation* on Maya's services on "Lemurian Code Healing" and "Infinite Cosmic Records," send an email to lemuriancodehealing@gmail.com, from her website.

Find Maya at: www.MayaTheShaman.com

2

THE ASSIGNMENT

BY: LORI THAYER. PH.D.

The Persecuted Healer

*A*s I lay on the couch in a state of facilitated hypnosis — my first experience — I immediately went to a past life where I saw myself in tattered clothes standing under a tarp deep in a patch of New England woods (circa mid-century/the 1600s). I stirred up a bowl of collected plants, fungi, and seeds as I sang and chanted over my secret potion in preparation for my next client. They would skulk quietly and sheepishly along a hidden path to my cabin door to seek relief of some seemingly incurable ailment. They only came in nervous desperation when they could not regain health from the apothecary of a licensed doctor's black bag; coupled with a serendipitous whisper from a neighbor or acquaintance providing landmark directions to my doorstep. I was a middle-aged indigent woman living on the edge of a small town, living off homemade root stew with maybe a small piece of animal fat mixed in for protein, acquired as an offering for my healing services. It was a rather lonely, desolate life, yet the nature spirits kept me company and comforted me in a soulful way. I somehow knew this life was an important assignment on planet Earth and I was here to help introduce and advance the practice and acceptance of "magical" healing. I also foresaw my future demise, yet I felt a calling to help anyone who came to my hearth to my very last day.

I could see innumerable details of the scene, including a dusty leather-bound almanac, sitting on a nearby tree stump, filled with long-practiced herbal remedies, tincture recipes, and directives for casting spells. I usually mixed my concoctions outside to absorb the energies of the sun's rays, moonlight, or starlight that beamed down into the bowl. Yet, I also knew that the potions I offered to my clients served more as a placebo than an organic remedy. People were too skeptical to accept the efficacy of healing energies. So by handing them a cup of something to swallow, they could more readily believe in (i.e., literally "swallow") the possibility of healing. Sometimes people would come to ask me to cast a spell, in which case I would produce talismans from nature, such as feathers, animal bones, sticks, and stones. I heartily granted benevolent spells, such as finding love; but for "evil" spells, I transmuted my clients' malevolent desires to inflict harm on another into visions of benevolent outcomes for themselves. I knew dark energy vibrated at a much lower frequency and therefore could not be supported by the light from the sun, moon, or stars. But I also knew that unhealed dark forces in humanity existed and that I would one day succumb to them.

Fast-forwarding to my final days, I was approached by two town officials who toted me away to the local jail to face my non-juried conviction of being a witch. In a dark, dank space with only a narrow wooden plank to sit upon, I prayed for humanity; knowing that each time healing was offered, a few more rays of light would seep into closed, hardened hearts. The next day I was led to the village gallows, where townspeople gathered to ogle and cheer on the death of yet another perceived demonic sorcerer in their midsts. Fortunately, by the time the noose was lassoed around my neck, I had already left my *body and watched on, like a moviegoer, a physical shell of myself ingesting a last waning breath. And then I was back floating in a light, misty space to review the life I had just experienced; and receive my next assignment. Damn — planet Earth again!?*

The Pandemic

Notably, the title of this section conjures up our experience with the coronavirus. Yet I am actually referring to the pandemic of an ongoing global-wide practice of condemnation of alternative healing practices (and practitioners) that do not fit into the profit-driven, allopathic medical establishment. Since the time of witch hunts, and long before, denigration and denial of the right to practice have dominated the mainstream response to various modes of natural healing. Authoritative medical organizations have long denounced mystical and non-materialist healing practices, including shamanism, herbalism, midwifery, and homeopathy, to name just a few. And now, the development and mind-control marketing of covid "vaccines" by colluding governing authorities with Big Pharma and the media has brought the censorship of alternative healing to a tipping point.

In the initial stages of covid awareness, as global case numbers and the death rate reportedly rose, people anxiously looked toward authoritative sources for answers. Meanwhile, various practitioners began to explore different remedies to prevent and treat this mercurial virus. Compounds such as Hydroxychloroquine and Ivermectin, as well as Vitamin D and other supplements, were found to be highly effective as prophylactics and early treatments — but their reported efficacy was soon squashed even before the vaccines were rolled out. Once covid "vaccines" became available, mainstream media outlets eradicated any information that questioned their safety and efficacy. Naturopaths, homeopaths, herbalists, and other non-allo-pathic healers, along with a small number of outspoken M.D.s and researchers, were ridiculed, maligned, and even threatened.

The censorship of information has become so blatant, and yet often without question by the public. Many individuals have become dulled to our waning freedoms of speech and choice for what's best for our bodies. People have been disempowered in their belief in and practice of their own ability to heal them-selves. Our inalienable health freedoms are being chipped away daily. This is the true pandemic! Thus, in actuality, the rise — and "fall-out" of the coronavirus may be a necessary event to wake more of us up finally!

The Power of One's Innate

People are being bombarded with pharmaceutical advertise-ments (the pharmaceutical industry presently the most powerful governmental lobby and biggest media sponsor). One's sense of personal responsibility and belief in self-healing is being under-mined. Most people fail to realize that their body has an innate system to keep them healthy and support them in healing. From time to time, people may need medical care for acute situations (broken bones, emergency appendectomies, etc.), but we have an internal healing system to maintain our health and well-being, to keep our immune system strong, and our cellular function optimal; thus reducing chronic diseases. Supporting our innate through a healthy lifestyle and honoring our innate through respectful communication are powerful ways to activate it. When we speak to our innate in the same way we might lovingly coddle a child or good friend, we activate our cellular system to repair, cleanse, balance, energize, and optimize its biological function. Every day I speak to my innate, thanking it for its collaborative effort to keep me healthy. Remember — Your innate within you is your "undying" partner.

Quantum Energy Healing

Astronomically, more light is now radiating onto our planet. And with this greater light energy, we have the opportunity to raise the energetic frequencies of our bodies. We can both shine this light inward and connect more deeply into our inner divinity; as well as shine this light out to humanity and Gaia. As we enhance the light energy of our bodies, over time we will need to depend less and less on physical tools and medicinals. At some point in the future, we will be able to tap into our healing process without the need for any physical formulation or manipulation. I do not know when that future time will come, but the more we focus on its possibility, the sooner it will arrive.

With the advent of the internet, it seemed that more and more people gained access to various healing techniques and remedies through online research. People could begin to take charge of their health and healing path in new and various ways. But online censorship has interfered with this process.

Yet, an interesting twist to all of this is playing out. As directives for social distancing, masking, and vaccination were enacted globally, more and more healers quickly developed online and remote access healing practices. More healers and clients realized and opened to the possibility of long-distance healing. I was one of those healers.

While I offered remote sessions in the past, I generally preferred in-person sessions, feeling them to be more powerful and authentic. I was more confident in my practice when I could feel the person's energy through physical proximity. If I had a remote session lined up, I felt more anxious about effectively reaching into the quantum field to access information and maneuver energy. But I, like many other healers, have quickly adapted and found an ability and beauty to working in the quantum realm.

Working remotely forced me to reach deeper into the quantum realm where I found a multilayered richness of information and insight that can better support my client in a multifaceted way. Once a healer feels more adept at virtually entering a multidimensional space, they can work more expansively — either remotely or in person. The gift is realizing that social distancing does not have to create a limiting barrier, but in some respects, has served as a gateway and catalyst to a deeper non-physical, non-linear means of connection!

Polarization

Every person on the planet is experiencing some form of polarization that accentuates a divide among humanity. This often plays out in politics, race relations, economics, and now a divide between the haves and have nots like no other — those that have had a shot and those that have not. Even relatives and friends are finding themselves on contentious opposing sides.

But the more profound polarization that I would like to highlight is between those who are opening up their hearts to let in a greater light, and those who are closing their hearts off to hold in the darkness; those who are opening to compassion even in the face of disagreement, and those shutting down with entrenched absolutes. We are in an evolutionary moment of duality between light and dark on this planet like never before. We have entered a galactic time-space continuum when the dark gets darker, and the light gets lighter. And since dark cannot exist where there is light, we know which force will eventually prevail. But we each must make a conscious choice in the degree of luminosity that we let in and ultimately radiate outward.

Opening your heart to self-love and then sending it out to others is critical for your well-being and everyone you encounter. Those who deny self-love and compassion hold on to a denser state of being, vibrating at a lower frequency. Inviting in light energy that is entering our planet's biosphere will raise one's frequency, supporting physical, mental, and spiritual health. Disease vibrates at a very low frequency, so when we vibrate at a higher frequency, we naturally inhibit germs and viruses from entering our bodies. This in itself is a powerful means to maintaining a healthier body (though at times disease may play a role in our soul's growth). When we vibrate at a higher frequency, we also attract other humans who vibrate at our level and thus engender healthier relationships. And when we vibrate at a very high frequency, we open ourselves to greater contact with our guides and the Masters.

Now is the Time

Whether you are just starting your healing journey to regain better physical and emotional health or continuing to deepen your spiritual growth — wherever you may be in your process — now is the time to shift into high gear! It doesn't matter where you are starting from — what matters is where you are focused on going and growing. We all come into the world with karmic wounds, and we all have likely suffered from our childhood in one way or another. So now is the time to begin or continue the healing, and most importantly, find a way to forgive others and forgive ourself for whatever hurts we carry. Through the process of forgiveness, we can regain or find a new sense of self-love and self-worth, which supports our ability to connect to a deeper level of compassion for other beings on the planet.

My Story

With a hard push down the birth canal and onto planet Earth again, I entered this life experience with innate regard for Gaia and the spirits of the earth, but a total lack of awareness of my connection to Source (which every person possesses). With agnostic and somewhat emotionally challenged parents, I had to circuitously navigate my way back to my inner spiritual world. Nature has always supported me on my path, yet a deep sense of emptiness always gnawed at my insides. It wasn't until I reached my late twenties that I met my first healer who helped me open the door to an inward emotional awareness. From that point, I began to crave healing at a deeper and deeper level, continually meeting more healers who offered a variety of alternative modalities. And with each crevice of darkness that I filled with light, I more readily connected with my guides.

I then began to attend all kinds of workshops and trainings to learn various modes of healing. After years of study and exploration, with great trepidation (having been persecuted for this vocation many past lives), I opened my healing practice in 2014. I named my practice "Stargate Garden" to evoke the profound and powerful connection between the Cosmic and the earth plane (and at the time, I happened to live on a street named Glengarden). As I continue to expand my knowledge-base of healing processes, I've also been able to enhance my "intuition-base." My ongoing discoveries -- often in the form of downloads — have helped me to more readily reach into the quantum field. It's a never ending exploration with myriad dimensional layers to mine, making it all the more exciting, dynamic — and daunting.

Your Story

Whether fully aware — or just awakening to the realization that we've entered a critical planetary period, I hope you will feel a call to heal. Many paths lead to a healthier body and an emotionally "light"-hearted state of being. There are many modalities to choose from and many healers available to guide you in your process. So I encourage you to explore different possibilities and find the healing approach and person who resonates with your needs and goals. It may be one or maybe many. Please don't stagnate in pain and darkness, anger, fear, frustration, or any other low vibrational emotion. If you desire to open up to the light and "enlighten" your load, ask for assistance. Whether seeking other humans and/or your spiritual guides, you will be supported in your first/next steps. This is your assignment — if you choose to accept it. It's your choice!

Sayings:

"Doctors treat the body, but Energy Healers treat the Soul. And everything stems from the soul's well-being."

— **Radhaa Nilia**

LORI THAYER, PH.D.

ABOUT THE AUTHOR

Thayer, Ph.D., began studying reiki and energy healing in the mid-1990s, followed by training in shamanic healing, spiritual counseling, metaphysics, channeling, hypnotherapy, and medical intuition. In 2009, Lori received her Ph.D. in anthropology from the University of Massachusetts at Amherst upon completing her dissertation, entitled "The Adoption of Shamanic Healing into the Biomedical Health Care System in the United States."

In 2014, Lori opened her practice, Stargate Garden Healing Center (www.stargategarden.com), to offer in-person (and more recently remote) healing sessions that combine her varied skills to support a client's healing at the soul level.

3

BUTTERFLY HEALING

BY: PATRICIA HOPKINS

This is the story of how Butterfly Healing came into my life and a description of the Butterfly Healing System™ that I developed as a result of this magical journey that I now use to serve my clients.

My Butterfly Healing Medicine Journey

I discovered I had a deep calling to use my hands for healing touch. It awakened in me in my mid-30s when I had a "gap," a still-point in my life caused by an emotionally traumatic event. As a result, a part of me that had been deeply asleep woke up, and I decided without any doubts to take a leave of absence from my environmental health job to go to a healing arts school and train as a massage therapist.

We are all healers. Like me, some of us just get called to go deeper into a vocation with it. To fulfill a desire to master certain skills and aspects for service to the collective.

When I was younger, I always picked up on everybody's

energies, and I often found that I had to sit far apart from people because it overwhelmed and confused my own energy system. I always wondered why I didn't hang out in big groups of friends. I would go for a bit, and then I had to leave for a period of time to find myself again. It often left me feeling like I didn't belong anywhere. I found that when people felt pain or were scared, I felt it in my body, and I was confused by it and would avoid being around disconcerting events and situations because I didn't know how to deal with the feelings. I was frightened by the intensity of what I could feel from others, which often made me feel depressed because I didn't know how to discern my feelings from others.

In my adult years, I worked to develop and master my empathic gift to allow me to fully show up in my ability to know exactly what people need to balance their systems and to know exactly what a room needs to bring balance to the energy and create a sacred and safe space.

I believe that through Spirit in the form of an archetypal being called the Metamorphix, the Butterfly Medicine Woman (The Alchemical Priestess), I created the Butterfly Healing System™ of vibrational medicine to share with the world. She began coming to me in my meditation and journey time about 11 years ago, and I began my journey of learning different healing modalities, including bodywork, energy healing, and spiritual healing and transformation. The purpose of this journey with Her has been to liberate me from the limitations of my mind that were created by collective consciousness and my individual karma. She came to liberate my authentic luminous self to support others in the same way.

In the beginning, I never knew how this was all going to come together, but I knew in my bones that it would. Now I see the work as a master alchemist who creates a specific blend of

Butterfly Medicine for each person to help them harmonize their system as they expand into their authentic soul essence. It is an intuitive method implemented with mastery in many modalities.

I believe that the Butterfly Healing System™ came to me in this life as a culmination and celebration of the wisdom from many past lives of being a healer, medicine woman, and alchemist. I have had many past life traumas cleared over the last seven years through my Akashic Records work wherein every single life I was persecuted, exiled, ostracized, burned, poisoned, beheaded, hung, tortured, or buried alive because of the alchemical medicine that my soul has always brought to Earth to share.

It goes beyond that into my cosmic life, where I have often been a messenger and a carrier of peace and harmony codes as a cosmic grid worker. Here on Earth, I serve as an Earth grid worker, an Emissary of Sacred Earth, and I've always carried energy in codes in my body as vibrations from one place to another. I still am responsible for multi-dimensional and inter-stellar travel in this lifetime. Basically, I am a Light being, a tuning fork for higher frequency consciousness here on Earth. That is my job to adjust other systems to do the same.

My clients have been able to find healing and transformation with this modality by accessing new neural and energetic pathways for living their lives by shifting their system's energies to align with higher frequency lifestyle earth and cosmic grids. It brings me great peace and joy to see others find a way to love themselves deeply and find joy and satisfaction in their lives.

I have fallen in love with this system over and over because it brings me great pleasure to indulge my clients in the highest frequency of their senses to reach a high energetic shift that climaxes as a breakthrough in the field of armor, blocking the luminosity of their true soul essence and opening them up to experiencing a life that is deeply rooted in that authenticity and thus is much more satisfying and nourishing for them.

This system is so unique because it is the magical crucible of the Metamorphix. It is a cauldron vibrational medicine where She is guided to achieve the desired mixture of frequencies needed to address the imbalances in the concern system.

I frequently find that the client will come in with fragmented and frenetic energy in these sessions. However, once they drop into that sacred deep zone of Metamorphosis, they find that still point of death and rebirth, and when they emerge from this sacred cocoon with a completely different energy signature. They stand taller, their bodies stand relaxed and steady, and their eyes bright with Light and new life. Everything is aligned and magnifies their authentic soul essence.

One of the most amazing sessions is when someone has a breakthrough, and they start to speak Light language, and it just changes the whole chemistry of their body in an instant. These moments of cracking the vessel are miraculous to me and represent the highest Light resonating sessions of sacred and magical phenomena.

After a series of sessions, I witness clients bubbling over with newfound joy and talking of newfound freedoms in their lives. This is in such contrast to how they showed up initially, shut down physically, emotionally, mentally, and spiritually, speaking only of the stress in their lives. I love it when they begin to acknowledge the positive changes in themselves and notice the beauty of things around them for the first time. Their awareness is completely expanded in their appreciation for the beauty of their own blessed life.

I truly want to bring this work forward into the world in a really magical yet accessible way. I want to bring it out to reach people who really need transformation because they are so locked into limiting patterns that need to be unwound.

I want to bring it to people in a healing sanctuary space that I have dreamed of creating for many years. It is a center for healing and transformation where offering sessions in person will be key. The hands-on presence and the ability to use touch, sound, crystals, and movements are true art and celebration of Butterfly Healing. It really is about taking people deep into that sacred Metamorphosis with the Metamorphix present for the entire time and basically coordinating the whole session through me.

I plan to train other people to use this method and create a certification program for Alchemical Healing and Transformation with the Butterfly Healing System™. I want to make this accessible to the general public, and I also want to work with leaders and use this system to sharpen and refine their energy systems, so they can step out in a more profound way in whatever they do in service to the world.

I want people to have amazing experiences that change how they see reality without altering them using chemicals besides the plant allies of the essential oils. So that's my dream to offer these in person at the sanctuary or on retreats in sacred spaces and places worldwide as initiations for Emissaries of Sacred Earth and the Ecstatic Leaders and Peacekeepers.

I also want to offer this work for people in transition to help them cross over and transition peacefully into the Light. I don't know when that part of my work as a myrrhaphore, midwife of death will come allowing me to work in the Magdalene mysteries, but I do know that is part of it all.

For now, I am here to help others be released from old paradigm limitations and provide initiations for those who want to step into a priestess or emissary role in 5D leadership. I am also here for those that want to access the other worlds and dimensions to access their Cosmic or Divinity Codes.

My work in this world is clearing out resistance in the body energetically in the cells to receive the upgrades needed to evolve into a luminous Light being.

The Butterfly Healing System™

The Butterfly Healing System is a Portal to Total Metamorphosis and Transformation of your Life.

The Butterfly Healing System is a framework of high-frequency vibrational medicine for the body, mind, and soul. The System works directly with your energy field and cellular matrix to clean, clear, and realign your system to higher frequency life force levels.

The therapist works directly with the client's energy field to support the activation of higher frequency energies within the cellular matrix that have been dormant for various reasons. The shift in the energy body allows the physical body to come into a new set point where the sympathetic nervous system is not stuck in the "on" position producing stress chemicals and the associated physical milieu of aliments. The energetic shift allows the body's DNA to turn "on" the process for producing the nurturing and nourishing chemistry in the physical body associated with safety, pleasure, and joy balancing out the stress chemicals, so they are only produced when needed to react to a true threat. The newfound energy can be used for creativity and love. It also supports the client to direct strong emotions into creativity as part of the process. Even the heavier emotions and trauma that are a part of life are filled with gems of inspiration and can be excavated for the client's benefit.

Sessions may be similar, yet no one is exactly the same.

However, there is a basic framework for each session. First, the therapist opens the Akashic Field or Records of the client at the beginning of each session to support the alignment of the tools used for the session and may use an Oracle Card Reading to set the intention for the session. The work with the Akashic Records taps into the metamorphic field and accesses the power to clear and rewrite the client's energy field to a higher frequency timeline. Next, the physical body is addressed with a combination of hands-on healing, including gentle massage, cranio-sacral therapy, crystal therapy, and Aromatherapy for the health of the tissues of the physical body to clear, balance, and activate the physical body. Next, healing of the emotional body is addressed utilizing the essential oils, sound (tuning forks, singing bowls, drum, and rattle), and light language. Finally, the spiritual body is addressed using essential oils, sound, light language, Reiki, and a library of metaphysical attunements to cosmic and divine frequencies to expand consciousness. Gene Key, Human Design, and astrology information may be provided to the client upon request. I love to use these additional tools to help clients see the beauty and true divinity of their soul essence and the mechanics of the human vehicle they chose in this incarnation.

There are two ways to receive from the System:
Butterfly Body Healing & Butterfly Energy Healing

1.) Butterfly Body Healing

This in-person session is a fusion of Alchemical Aromatherapy, Cranio-sacral Therapy, Crystal Therapy, Guided Energy Healing Meditation, Light Language Healing, Massage, Reiki Healing, Sound Healing, Oracle Reading, and Creating Sacred Space.

1. Alchemical Aromatherapy uses essential oils from plants to alter mood, cognitive function, or health.

2. Cranio-Sacral Therapy is a gentle yet powerful technique that effectively releases body pain and mental stress by optimizing the movement of cerebrospinal fluid.

3. Crystal Therapy is the practice of placing crystals with appropriate healing properties on a client's body to support the session.

4. Guided Energy Healing is a guided visualization healing process for the client utilizing Violet Flame, Crystal Rose, Rainbow Sequence Healing, Orb of Life, Ho'oponoponoHo'oponopono, and other metaphysical techniques appropriate for the session to release old habits that keep you stuck in physical, emotional, and spiritual pain and suffering.

5. Light Language Healing uses the therapist's voice to create nonverbal sounds that emit a frequency the client needs for healing.

6. Massage utilizes gentle pressure and strokes using the therapist's hands, arms, or feet appropriate for the client's head, body, and feet to release tension and stimulate circulation for healing for the client.

7. Reiki Healing utilizes Usui & Karuna Reiki, a Japanese

form of energy work that cleanses and balances the energy system in the body. As a result, the body's natural self-healing mechanisms strengthen, helping to establish optimum health.

8. Sound Healing uses tuning forks, singing bowls, rattles, and drums to create the vibrations frequencies the client needs for healing.

9. Oracle Reading uses various oracle card decks and the Akashic Field & Records to help identify the issue, the tool, and the potential outcome for the healing session.

10. Creating Sacred Space uses Feng shui and Vastu vidya elements and interior design to create space in the client's home or workplace to support their healing after the session.

2.) Butterfly Energy Healing Session

The main difference between Butterfly Body Healing and Butterfly Energy Healing is that the latter includes all tools and techniques, except alchemical Aromatherapy, cranial-sacral therapy, or massage. See Butterfly Body Healing Session for the description of tools and techniques.

Sayings:

"As you keep on doing your healing work, you influence others to heal as well. Our world shifts one healing at a time!"

—Radhaa Nilia

PATRICIA WALD-HOPKINS

ABOUT THE AUTHOR

Patricia Wald-Hopkins is a Modern Mystic, Infinite Self Catalyst,
and Soul Liberation Guide for those ready to break free from old

paradigm limitations and awaken to the gifts of their Infinite Self, so they can lead the life they are DIVINELY designed to live. She supports her clients as an Akashic Records Wisdom Guide and with various healing and transformational modalities, including essential oil perfumes, crystals, and light language to support them to embody their Infinite Self. She is a Gene Keys Ambassador and Guide and a co-founder of the School of Light, a mystery school based on Gene Keys transmission. She is the author of a chapter, The EmBODY Codes: Transmissions of a Mystic on the Sacred Body and Being Human, in the book Sacred Body Wisdom: Igniting the Flame of Our Divine Humanity; the author of the chapter, The Miracle of Light Language: Awakening to My Soul Voice and Purpose, in the book Miraculous, and the creator of the Infinite Self Oracle Card deck.

Patriciawaldhopkins.com

4

UNSTOPPABLE HEALING

BY: LESLIE ALLYN FINKEL

My Accidental Awakening

It was spring 2008, a day not unlike most others. I'd worked many hours at the Phoenix Police, maintaining critical computer systems, putting out fires, and ever-developing new systems. Then, as I did every day, I drove in heavy traffic on the five-lane freeway to my house that I was renovating. Everything seemed calm. Traffic was bumper to bumper moving about 20 miles an hour. BAM!

As my head and torso went flying backward, I looked in the rearview mirror to see this huge commercial truck crashing into me. Everything around me was in slow motion. I hadn't braked or anything, so it took me by total surprise. The funny thing was, I didn't feel any pain. It was later that night I realized I had been in shock. The next day, unbearable pain started to flood my body.

The next nine months were a never-ending nightmare. I relentlessly sought out physical therapy, massage therapy, and chiropractic care. On top of that, I had a year-long lawsuit against my insurance company because they only offered me $150 for my pain, suffering, and damages.

My chiropractor explained that I had suffered extreme whiplash, and the S curve in my neck was gone. It had no spring whatsoever. So I did what I always do. I became unstoppable and devoted myself to all these therapies in the hope of going back to being as active and athletic as I had been before the accident.

Over time, my neck and back got somewhat better. However, I still had a nagging ache in my lower back. I was getting despondent as I started thinking I might have to live like this for the rest of my life. What else could I do but cry out to the universe for help?

Just when I thought I would have to live with this chronic pain forever, salvation came in an unexpected visit from a Tibetan Dakini who also happened to be a master Chi Nei Tsang teacher and practitioner. Khadro was a long-time friend of my wife whom she'd studied with years ago.

My wife swore up and down that the healing she had experienced was nothing short of a miracle. She urged me to get a Chi Nei Tsang treatment from Khadro. I had no idea what it was, but I was at the point where I was willing to try anything to get fully over the pain. However, hiring a "healer" was a foreign idea to me. All I ever knew was to go to a doctor.

Destiny Calls

Khadro kneeled next to me as I lay on the floor. She started by putting her hand on my belly. I didn't understand what she was doing, but it felt okay, maybe even a little relaxing. The next day I woke up, I noticed that I still had backache.

So I asked Khadro for a second session. It was in this second session that, for the first time in my life, I felt this incredible sensation I can only describe as "warm molasses pouring in all directions in my back." It felt heavenly.

I said, "what in the world am I feeling, Khadro?" She went on to tell me that it was energy flowing, that I'd had a massive energy block which she was able to free up. She reestablished the Chi flow, which had been disrupted for all of those nine months.

As I stood up in jubilation, free from the pain I'd been living with for so long, Khadro asked me a question that took me by as much surprise as did the original accident. She asked, "why were you a match to being hit by that truck?" I looked at her like she was crazy and said, "what are you talking about? I was just driving along, minding my own business, and BOOM, this truck crashed into me. It was shitty luck, that's all."

She asked me again why I was a match to being hit by that truck. Then she asked me if there were other cars around me. I answered, "yes, there were cars all around me." She said, "So why do you think the truck hit you and not anyone else?"

Now I consider myself a fairly open-minded person, but this way of thinking was foreign to me. Nonetheless, I decided to entertain her question as I began ruminating about that traumatic day. I remembered that I'd had a horrible argument with my ex-wife. I spent the whole afternoon trying to put it out of my mind so that I could just be calm and get on with my day.

Boy, was my mind blown. Khadro had planted a seed in my awareness that my bottled-up anger and frustration had made me a magnet to the crash. Even more so, I was now open to the idea that we store all sorts of negative energies in our bodies and that if we don't process them, they can lead to chronic physical and emotional issues.

I decided right then and there that I wanted to learn this healing modality, "Chi Ni Song?" so I could bring incredible relief to others. It was a crazy idea to me because, since the age of 28, I had made a plan to work for 26 years in my career in the city, retire at 54, and become a high school math teacher. Boy did my life change forever!

I started traveling to Canada for four years to study at Khadro's School of Chi Nei Tsang. I finished my city career in 2016 and launched my long-awaited passion of having my own practice called Unstoppable Healing™.

What Is Chi Nei Tsang?

Chi Nei Tsang is a thousands-year-old healing modality. It came out of the ancient treasure chest of White Cloud monks, descending from Taoist and Tai healing and meditation practices. Chi Nei Tsang is a comprehensive method of detoxifying, energizing, and rejuvenating vital organs and their surrounding fascia, a much-ignored phenomenon by modern medicine. Fascia is a white web-like network that wraps around all organs, muscles, bones, and nerves - therefore referred to as Interconnective Tissue.

The philosophy behind Chi Nei Tsang is that people's internal body systems are perfectly correlated to their outer physical world and even the universe. Each organ is mapped to one of the five elements - Fire, Earth, Metal, Water, and Wood. If you think about the relationships between these elements, you can understand that the same exists for all organs. Each organ holds different emotional energy. For example, the liver holds anger, the kidneys and bladder hold fear, and the stomach holds worry. Recognize the saying, "I'm so worried I have a knot in my stomach."

The White Cloud Monks also determined the specific frequencies of healthy organs and mapped correlating sounds and colors to bring ailing organs back into equilibrium. They incorporated these healing frequencies into meditative poses to maintain optimal health.

To me, there's no better way to achieve the highest level of emotional wellbeing and renewed joy while releasing unhealthy, stagnant patterns and revitalizing all of your body systems from the inside out. No drugs. No talk therapy. No side effects.

Put Your Mind In Time Out

Many people come to me after trying other healing modalities, including Chiropractic, Physical Therapy, Acupuncture, and even Talk-Therapy. Most suffered from an unGodly amount of emotional trauma, ranging from physical and verbal abuse to horrible relationships, losing loved ones, and a plethora of stressful situations and events.

I allow you to unload fully in your first Unstoppable Healing session. It helps build a trusting relationship between us. I've found that my listening caringly supports you to go deeper into your subconscious during the rest of the session. Eventually, I tell you to put your mind in "timeout" or the "penalty box."

Then I take you on an energetic journey into your body. With your eyes closed, you'll be on a powerful, even vivid discovery, unlike anything you've experienced before - being led right to the root of where your emotional and physical issues hide so that you can process and toss them away forever.

I rub my palms together to create warmth and Chi flow before I energetically scan your abdomen. Then I gently use various rolling and spiraling massage strokes, loosening your surface fascia before moving into your deeper fascia and then towards your organs. While doing this, I look for inflammation, rashes, lumps, cysts, fibroids, shallow or difficult breathing, and much more.

I also check for denseness, hardness, and any unusual color changes while observing any heat, cold, moisture, or dryness emanating from your skin. I've often put my hand on a person's belly, and it was as cold as ice in one area yet warm in others. I've even seen energy vortexes come out of peoples' livers. I discern from these observations which elements and organs are out of balance.

I focus greatly on your breathing, having your first breath into your belly and then your chest, exhaling in reverse. Breathing in this fashion allows your organs to come down, creating space for your diaphragm to expand while enhancing peristaltic motion in your transverse colon. This loosens any physical or energetic clogs or blockages in your digestive tract, lymph, and meridian systems.

Your navel is where your birth energy is stored. This is where all energy flowed while your mother carried you into this world, and it remains a central Chi source during your life. If your navel is off-center or has knots or "line pulls" (where organs or body systems have siphoned energy), I will balance it before proceeding to the organs that may be energy deficient.

Incredibly, everyone has what's called "Chi Balls" around their navel, which feel like ping pong balls underwater. I press on them until they pop, dispersing stored energy for renewal and repair. Miraculously, the Chi Balls replenish their energy until needed again.

I work with your organs and fascia tissues on all levels – physically, emotionally, and spiritually – to make them work more efficiently and heal from unprocessed negative emotions that you may have unknowingly carried throughout your life. As part of this attunement process, we even clear limiting energy imprints inherited from parents, family lineage, and past lives.

What You Experience

Most people I've worked with share similar experiences generated during our Unstoppable Healing sessions. They feel sensations of electricity or fire, see a myriad of colors, images of people or scenes, and most importantly, exude powerful emotions of sadness, grief, anger, or anxiety.

I remain aware of how their body moves, the sounds they make, and changes to their breathing pattern to help guide them through the process. Sometimes they wail, sob, swear or scream. Other times they feel like they fell asleep. In reality, they're on the edge of a subconscious drift. They are mostly unaware that their fingers, toes, and legs move and twitch every way.

A healing shift can occur at any time during or even in the days after receiving a Chi Nei Tsang treatment. There may be momentary discomfort or pain as you let go of buried painful emotions. Miraculously, the discomfort disappears just as swiftly as it came about.

It's my highest intention for you to feel safe and protected at all times. Though I do not know what you're processing, I'm a sensitive empath and use my intuition and higher guidance. I'm also your champion, protector, and coach all at once. That's why I won't let you run away and avoid whatever is coming up for you, so you're able to let it go for good.

Incredible Client Stories

Now that I've painted you a picture, I will share three of the hundreds of incredible client stories I've been honored to witness over the years.

I gave Chi Nei Tsang to the wife of a couple who had been trying to conceive a child for several months to no avail. In our first session, she felt a "black veil" lifting off of her female organs. Two weeks later, she told me she was pregnant! She sensed that the "black veil" stemmed from energy in her family lineage.

Next, a woman told me she'd been rear-ended three times while stopped at intersections and now suffers from panic attacks anytime she stops at one. She even started being scared to leave her house. Can you believe she drove over 1-1/2 hours each way for her three Unstoppable Healing sessions?

Months later, I happened to check in with her. She shared that after her three sessions, she not only permanently lost her panic attacks and fear of leaving her house, she experienced an unexpected bonus healing! She confided that her heart had been broken several times over the years and that she'd walled off her heart. Now that her entire world had opened up, she was ecstatic to have started a long-term relationship with a man!

During my training in Canada, I gave Chi Nei Tsang to a 71-year-old psychotherapist from Nova Scotia. While I detoxified her liver, she started to twist her head from side to side. She frantically repeated, "is my neck broke!" I told her "no" and kept assuring her that she was safe. This continued for several minutes as she gradually returned to the "real" world.

She shared a most incredible story, telling me that she climbed a ladder to where her dad worked on the second story of the house he was building when she was only four. She fell, and her dad came flying down the ladder screaming at her because he thought she was dead. Well, she'd fallen onto a flower bed he'd just planted, and she had nearly a scratch! I was blown away that she'd stored such a painful memory in her body for an entire lifetime without consciously knowing!

You Can Free Yourself

I can't emphasize enough that Chi Nei Tsang addresses the "Whole You." Besides eliminating pains, aches, toxins, and psychological and emotional stress, it is a mystical modality for modern-day sleep, digestive, and nervous disorders, such as PTSD, anxiety, and depression.

Chi Nei Tsang speeds up recovery from injury or trauma and is known for its healing success with endometriosis, fertility, or sexual issues for women and men. It also helps autoimmune diseases such as Lupus and chronic fatigue syndrome.

The bottom line is that you will feel a greater ability to tackle whatever life throws your way. Furthermore, it increases your overall vibration, leading to higher quality experiences. That's why it's no surprise that my clients change jobs and relationships after our sessions. Many also say they are now aware of their emotional triggers and can better handle stressful situations with vigor and flow.

No matter where you're in the world, I'm inviting you to learn more about the miraculous healing of Chi Nei Tsang and how you, too, can become unstoppable.

Remember, it's no accident you've read this chapter!

～

Sayings:

"When I discovered Healing, my life forever changed. It was the long winding path that would be an adventure of a lifetime."

— *Radhaa Nilia*

LESLIE ALLYN FINKEL

ABOUT THE AUTHOR

Leslie Allyn Finkel is on a mission to free people from their traumas, pains, and everyday stresses so they can thrive and enjoy their life to the fullest. He is the Founder of Unstoppable Healing™, where he leads clients to profound life and health changes using an ancient Taoist healing science called Chi Nei Tsang.

Leslie is passionate about helping people heal holistically

from the inside out. His clients report astounding results, whether relieving chronic pain from accidents and physical injuries, releasing emotional traumas and anxieties, or eliminating digestive and hormonal issues.

Leslie enjoyed a 30+ year career in Information Technology. He devoted 26 years to the City of Phoenix Police, where he proudly administered all mission-critical systems, including the 911 Emergency System.

He has a Bachelor in Mathematics and Computer Science from Tulane University and 25 combined years studying Chi Nei Tsang, Tai Chi, and Martial Arts.

Learn more at: Unstoppabablehealing.com/EnergyMedicine.

5

ANGEL

BY: AMANDA WATERMAN

I have always been an empath and could feel other people's emotions. I can read non-verbal communication a little more than is sometimes comfortable. I love to fix people's problems, and I love to problem solve before there is a problem, so it's only natural that I am a caregiver for work and my personal life. Throughout my life, I have been surrounded by addiction. I have always been in the background while I could hear others' judgments and opinions about how people who are stuck in addiction behave, how they act, and what bad choices they make. It always affected me when I would hear people talk and wonder why they couldn't see these individuals the way I could see them with love and compassion. Why couldn't they see all the pain and suffering? More importantly, why could I feel their sorrow at such a young age?

In 2018, I was introduced to The Emotion Code. I had a few sessions. These sessions changed my life and soon would change the lives of everyone around me. I had a huge yearning to heal myself. All of my older kids had substance abuse issues, and I knew that I couldn't continue to react to the craziness that they were creating in our lives. I was fascinated by everything I was learning and discovered that I decided to become a Certified Emotion Code Practitioner. Just learning kinesiology and how to do muscle tests changed my life. I found a tool that I could use to ask my higher-self questions. I started practicing with all of my friends. I would release their pains, headaches, sadness, whatever was coming up for healing. I believe that their souls knew what I was learning and that I could help them heal.

One day after I dealt with an emotional situation involving addiction, I heard a voice loud and clear say, "You're going to heal them!" That made perfect sense, But how? I knew I had to figure out the how part on my own. The next day was my first body code session with Marta. As I was on the zoom call with her and she had started my session, I had a divine download that this is what I was going to use to help heal those in addiction! I was amazed by what I saw on the screen and what was being divinely downloaded and shown. I could see how I could help. Ideas started rushing through my brain.

Soon after that, I created through prayer what I like to call my "Heart Wall Protocol." It started with releasing heart walls that Dr. Nelson teaches in the Emotion Code. Then I was divinely guided on what to add to this amazing protocol that has helped so many people so far, not just in addiction but in many other areas where people were suffering, including being stuck in their businesses or not being able to release the desired body weight. I have helped 100's of people release what they need. I have a Facebook group called Clear Coding with Amanda that I do free healing live. I have created an Addiction Protocol where I release miasms and generational curses causing addictions.

I have successfully become a Certified Emotion Code Practitioner, an Access Consciousness Bars Practitioner and Facilitator, Certified Life Coach, Founding Member of Global Strong, I lead Masterminds/Advisory Round Tables, Certified Ho'Oponopono Practitioner, Certified Angel Guide, Medium, Intuitive, an original 144,000 Twin Flame, and an Angel Activator.

Being an Angel Activator is one of the most important jobs I have, besides being a Twin Flame. I wasn't aware that I was an angel until my friend Colette invited me to an online event that she was having. Nigel, another angel activator, was there, and he said something to me that got my full attention. "Amanda, hasn't anyone told you that you were an angel?" I said, "Yes, but I'm a caregiver so my clients tell me that all the time." He said, "Then why don't you believe them?" I explained that I was just doing my job. He said, "No, you're not listening! Amanda, you are an angel!" I had to start waking up the other angels! With that knowledge and awareness, it sent me on a new trajectory.

Through my energy healing, I would start asking my client, "if I was working with an angel." Most angels chose to be born into a family with a lot of dysfunction and trauma. I have discovered that angels have Core Negative Beliefs that go directly against their divine purpose. During sessions, I start discovering what the core negative beliefs are. Most angels are so cute, and they have chosen many-core negative beliefs, "they are plain." You have to understand when angels choose to come to Earth; we have to fit in and blend in with everyone else. If we looked the most beautiful and had the most magnetism, we wouldn't be able to learn the life lessons we signed up for. At the end of a session with my angel clients, we create positive affirmations that remind them of who they are and their divine purpose. It is such a powerful experience, and it's amazing to see people stepping into their divine power. It is something that we create together, so they feel empowered. I was convinced that everyone was an angel until I came across one lady that wasn't. Then I remembered that all of my kids are angels except one of my daughters; she's a fairy. Fairy's come here to have fun. One thing that you can count on when being an energy healer is that you will learn something new every day and be open to other possibilities that you may not have been aware of previously.

Earth Angels tend to have a lot of demons attached to them. There are many different reasons for this. They could be attached to a trapped emotion. Each emotion has its own vibration, and the negative emotions that get trapped open a doorway for demons to attach themselves to you. It's so important to release negative trapped emotions. It's also important to keep your vibration as high as possible. I explain to my clients that when they drink alcohol or do drugs, it lowers their vibration allowing access to the demons to attach. Another reason Earth Angels have demons attached is "because they have a BIG purpose, and these demons would like to stop you." Lastly, a demon could be attached because, like me, they want you to transmute them. You could be a portal for them. We are the master creators when we are creating each of our lives, then we are born with the veil of amnesia from all our other lives and then add all of the contracts, vows, and promises that we have made. It gets really interesting to unravel it all.

Recently my son was in the hospital on life support, and I had to kick the demons out of his room and bring the life force energy up in his room to aid in his healing and then for the entire hospital. Demons usually attack me through my kids because they will get my attention. I do not believe that any demon is happy here doing the job that they signed up for, so I give them a choice to do something else. Shannon O'Hara, the step-daughter of Gary Douglas, founder of Access Consciousness, has written books about working with entities and I purchased and read her books, "Talk to the Entities" and "Beings of Light." She talks about her experience with entities and how she releases them by giving them a choice to choose something greater.

People in addiction are the brightest souls and had labels placed on them as children. Put on medication to calm them down enough to focus. It is my opinion the meds create more bad than good for the soul. The meds that are prescribed to these little kids are stimulants. When they age out of their parent's insurance and no longer have access to getting their prescription that they are already addicted to, they usually turn to the street to find an alternative, and most of them turn to drugs to try to feel normal. These souls are very high vibrational beings here to change the world and help us ascend, but the schools and teachers are not trained or equipped to support them.

I remember the day that my son's first-grade teacher told me that I needed to get him on medication. He was only six years old. I was a young single mom, attending college and working two jobs. I have a very impressive mind and listened to those I thought were the experts in their fields. I begged the doctor not to put him on meds, but the school said that if he wasn't put on meds, he couldn't attend. I was bullied like so many other parents. I wish I knew then what I know now. My son used to beg me not to send him to school. His little self-esteem was so poor. He was always such a hard sleeper, and I could not wake him up in time for school. Now I know that he was probably working hard in the astral world, then having to get up early and attend school for 8 hours was way too much for him to handle.

We may be too late to problem-solve before there's a problem, but as lightworkers and starseeds, it's never too late to find a solution and start over to help raise the collective consciousness. That is what we are here for. Am I doing this to answer my

WHY? My WHY is this... I am doing this for all the mama's out there that gave birth to a little soul with a huge purpose, and the world tried to beat them down and extinguish their light. I am doing this for all of my children who have lost their best friends and cousins to accidental overdoses and other traumatic deaths. I am doing this for all the kids who ended up in jail because they didn't know of a different way to live because they were born in the perpetual cycle of addiction. I am doing this for my family. In the depths of my soul, I know that I have been called to figure it out and bring it to humanity and the collective consciousness. It is what drives me every single day, every minute, wanting to figure it out. I do this to BE the light unto others.

One thing that keeps me on track is my Advisory Round Table at Global Strong--I have my meetings on Sundays because we talk about our goals and take steps to get there. If we get stuck, we have our very own board of directors that will help us brainstorm and give ideas. We have accountability partners that inspire us to keep going and not to give up on our big vision even when life is happening for us.

That brings me to my long-term goal to open up a holistic healing center. I have been on a quest to end the cycle of addiction. I have been guided for the last two years to go to Costa Rica and meet shamans or native medicine people that will help me on my journey and with my mission. I know while there that I will be "activated" in Costa Rica. I have no idea what that means or what I have to look forward to, but I am just following my inner knowing and my inner guidance. There is something special about the land and the native people there, and I am going there for a reason. There are no coincidences.

I didn't know about twin flames until I was activated in Las Vegas and was connected to my twin flame. My kundalini energy was on fire, and I had what I would call an out-of-body experience. I had no idea what was going on until I returned home to Seattle. Since then, I have been on a quest to find out the meaning of all of this and how my twin flame and I are to work together to help bring unconditional love and help raise the Earth's vibration to move into 5D. I know that we are part of the first wave of twin flames and part of the 144,000 chosen that the bible speaks of. I truly believe that we can do that by activating and healing the Earth angels stuck in addiction and raising their vibration and frequencies. Once we do this, it will be a ripple effect that will be felt throughout the world.

I was guided to a tent with crystals at a local fair. I found a "Blue Flame" Botryoidal Fluorite on Quartz, which was $144.00, and told the lady that I was taking the crystal home. She came over and was shocked that a particular crystal wanted to come home with me. She said this crystal is unique, and it's a huge transformation. I told her that I was going to Costa Rica on a retreat and knew that I would have a huge transformation the following week. Then she proceeds to tell me that the crystal holds Archangel Michael's energy in it. I said, "Really? My twin flame is Archangel Michael, and I am Lady Faith, so of course it wants to go home with me!" Even the price of $144.00 was a confirmation of who I am. I had been receiving the same message for a week, over and over. "Remember who you are!"

I want to leave you inner-standing that we are all connected, and for every emotion that we release, we release it for 350,000 other people. This domino effect is so powerful, and it keeps going. We can change the world one person at a time. Releasing negative energy raises the vibration that we need for the 5D world. I am committed to doing this. That is my mission and my purpose.

<u>Sayings:</u>

"Healing work is a sacred duty. To assist in helping heal others, makes our world a better place to live in."

—Radhaa Nilia

AMANDA WATERMAN

ABOUT THE AUTHOR

Everyone comes across with various types of challenges in their lives. Metaphysically speaking, these challenges come from other times in history, other points in time, and even other dimensions. Amanda Waterman has the gift to support you in healing and clearing these challenges so you can have the life you desire. As an Energy Healer, Angel Activator, Light Worker, Life Coach, Mastermind Leader, Addiction Advocate, and business owner, Amanda has a long list of skills and gifts to elevate your life on and at every level. She is selfless beyond words and somehow manages to give more than 100%, all while raising a family and caring for her senior clients.

Amanda is a Certified Emotion Code Practitioner, an Access Consciousness Bars Practitioner and Facilitator, Certified Life Coach, Founding Member of Global Strong, she lead Masterminds/Advisory Round Tables, Certified Ho'Oponopono Practitioner, Certified Angel Guide, Medium, Intuitive, an original 144,000 Twin Flame, and an Angel Activator.

www.clearcodingwithamanda.com

6

FINDING MY SUPERPOWER

BY: MISTY PENNINGTON

L ife is funny! I found my superpower when I stopped looking for it.

I was a number cruncher by trade, and retirement was on the horizon. It seemed like everything I had dreamt of and worked towards in my life was here. Yippee! That is what I thought I'd be feeling, yet something was missing.

My dad had passed away, my children had grown and started their own lives, good friends moved away, and grandkids were making their appearances. My relationships with everyone I loved seemed to be changing.

My health needed some attention; retiring gave me the time to work on the whole physical aspect of healing. I experienced the toll that dehydration, overuse, and poor nutrition had taken on my body, not to mention what multiple surgeries and a pretty serious motorcycle accident had contributed.

To celebrate my retirement, I traveled by myself to explore the International Gem and Mineral Show in Tucson, where I found Crystal Tones Alchemy Singing Bowls. I immediately fell in love. I couldn't explain what stirred the deeply euphoric feeling inside my heart. But on that crisp sunny Arizona day, I knew these singing bowls were going home with me and that something fascinating had occurred, even if I couldn't articulate it.

These beautiful tools were very expensive, and I was second-guessing if I SHOULD purchase them. I walked out of that tent with THREE bowls! There was just no way I could walk out of that tent without one of those bowls! So, I thought about how happy they made me feel and how retiring opened the door for fun things I loved to drop into my life.

It was a turning point for me to realize that I rarely made decisions independently. Before I did anything, I always consulted my husband, mother, sister, or considered everyone else that my decision would affect. It felt like everyone else, but I decided what I should do with my life.

I immediately felt tired of asking permission to live my life. I didn't need to justify my purchase to anyone. I texted my husband and warned, "I did a thing, don't be mad!" I followed it with a smiley face to try to soften it. That still makes me laugh when I think about it.

Before this moment, I was more focused on my husband's financial perspective than my own, and he surely felt like the financial supervisor in our relationship. Eww! We had created an energetic dynamic in our relationship from the awareness based on what we watched and learned from our parents and what seemed normal in society. Well, that wasn't going to work for me anymore.

And if I were 100% authentically and totally truthful, it felt like that dynamic had never 'worked.' We consistently had arguments about the power in our relationship. It seeped into every aspect of our life: raising our kids, our careers, finances, fun, and even sex.

In that short moment, I knew I must claim my own perspective.

In deciding to own my choice(s), I learned that I had been blaming others for the things I did or didn't do and for the things I thought I could or could not do. Clearly - I was playing the victim. Ouch.

As I started to live in this new place, I could see how many ways this pattern was woven into every aspect of our relationship. It was so deeply intertwined in my entire life, and while I knew that I couldn't do this one any longer, I also didn't know how NOT yet -- to do it.

I committed to being kind to myself and had to forgive myself if it was messy in learning how to change this pattern. Doing this also kept me accountable for not blaming anyone else for my behavior.

During a palm reading, I had recently learned that I have two rare blessings of creative energy deeply etched in the lines of my hands. I decided that was an opportunity to let my creativity shine in finding ways to live in these new awarenesses. If I wanted to do something different, I had the power to create it.

Even though I recognized that I was extremely creative, I often didn't express it effectively. Suppressing creativity had lent to a well-spring of effervescent energy within me. I was holding all my unique creativeness inside me - I wasn't expressing it.

I seem to be one of those who is always on the positive end of the scale regarding energy and feeling happy. And I am - but I have an extremely deep reservoir of feeling, and my threshold of feeling is high capacity.

Exploring this about myself has had a profound impact. I began to believe in myself and see myself in ways I could not before. Self-criticism, self-sabotage, and a lack of self-worth led to a deficit in self-confidence. I knew I was a good person, and somehow, I couldn't feel it.

I wanted to feel better about myself. I didn't say derogatory things about others. Why did I do this to myself?

Awareness is an amazing thing. When an expansion of awareness happens in our perspective, it usually creates ripples of expanded awareness in several areas of life. Sometimes the ripples are waves!

That one decision to honor my heartfelt tug to purchase the alchemy singing bowls led to more heartfelt explorations and expansions than I can tell you. They are still happening today - several years later!

In expansion mode, I began to look for people teaching sound healing or hosting sessions I could attend. I began to travel more frequently by myself, attending retreats to learn and experience more sound healing. I purchased more singing bowls. I discovered Reiki and became a certified Holy Fire/Usui and Karuna Reiki Master.

I spent several hours for several days, for weeks and months playing, singing bowls, and practicing Reiki, and realized an absolute connection between the Reiki symbols and how I heard the sound waves emitted by the singing bowls.

I didn't know what any of that meant. All I know is I heard it and felt it - and I loved the way it made me feel. Every time I hear singing bowls, my heart lifts, my spirit soars, and I become ever more present within the very moment in which I am living. The worries and woes of the past fade into quiet, and the dreams of future ideas no longer entice me into being distracted from what is right here and now.

I sit. I breathe. I feel. I get still. I am here.

Peace creeps over me like a warm blanket on a cool summer

evening. My facial muscles relax. My shoulders drop. Wow! How do singing bowls cause all of that to happen?

That's profound. I couldn't sit still before this.

I'm sure I would have been labeled ADHD in school today as a child.

I could run for hours and hours and hours and not be exhausted.

Every job I worked and left replaced my position with more than one person.

It's fair to say that I have A LOT of energy.

And, before I learned to slow down, I was in survival mode energetically and completely unaware of it.

I was people-pleasing every person I loved to the point of my own exhaustion - and I didn't even know it.

The ripple effect of that one decision highlighted so many ways I was showing up in my own life in an unaware perspective. I assumed I knew what others needed, and I showed up based on that knowledge. Which - isn't knowledge - it's an opinion. And it's judgmental. And short-sided.

OUCH. Hard realization - or EXPANDED AWARENESS...?

I intended to do these things for good reasons - because I loved every one of those people I did that for, and they became involved in that pattern with me. And suddenly, it didn't feel good to me to be in that pattern in my life anymore.

In. So. Many. Ways. Sigh.

Well, that's a lot of darn feelings to experience from playing some dang singing bowls. Right! The stillness created inside me has been a direct product of experiencing the song of these bowls. As a result, I'm a firm believer in these tools and their ability to relieve anxiety and reduce pain. If you are a seeker in the mysteries of life or an explorer of deep feelings, sound healing is one of the most supportive healing modalities you can embrace.

To me, music is the universal language for humankind. Every kind of music evokes a sense of feeling. It can make me cry, feel the urge to dance or tap my foot, or hum. Feelings expressed by instruments rarely need words to understand what is being conveyed.

I had zero music training before finding singing bowls. My favorite classes in school were art classes. I loved dancing and taught myself rhythm well enough to dance with the high school pom squad.

I LOVED expressing myself artistically - I felt the most confident with that type of expression. No wonder I felt disconnected working as a financial secretary, I wasn't horrible at it, but I wouldn't say I liked it. I did what I felt I had to do.

Retirement was really a gift, and now I was starting to sink into accepting it.

Let me emphasize - life is too short to do things you do not love for money. Sure, money is a currency in our culture. But every job can be done artistically, in beauty. When someone's heart is in their work, their work becomes ART.

I had found the space in my life where my art could become my work.

I created Reiki and sound-infused healing sessions and offered them to my family, friends, and colleagues. How I care for people could be delivered through Reiki. The song of my heart is played through my bowls. I am continually amazed by how sound healing affected me and those I was offering it to. I began to talk about it with everyone I knew.

I needed to share that something beautiful and simple existed to help us get through life with "more beauty and joy."

People interested in healing and self-care began asking if I would do this for them or play my bowls with some of their community offerings. I decided I would love to, and things started expanding rapidly!

I started playing my singing bowls with yoga and meditation teachers in the local community and decided to open my own healing room. In a short six months of doing this, I outgrew the space and needed more privacy. I expanded into a 650 square foot room. Within a year, I expanded to a 1,000 SF space.

Before long, people coming to my sessions wanted to purchase some of these bowls to use as their tools for transformation in their own lives or businesses, so I began purchasing more inventory to offer them for sale to my clients.

Most people want to live with an open, loving, and compassionate heart. My passion and superpower are creating a safe space for those who want to dive into the depths of their heart and to live more authentically from that space with increased compassion and love. The journey to living with vulnerability and softness is to learn to love ourselves.

When we love all parts of ourselves - especially the hurt and wounded parts of us that we usually don't want to own - our capacity to love others unconditionally for who they truly are, grows.

That one moment of honoring myself in the singing bowl tent has taught me all of that.

I love creating sound journeys for so many reasons: to enable a person to hear the whisper of their heart, relax more deeply, increase creativity, facilitate an emotional release, and many more reasons.

Sound healing has had a profound effect on my life. It has enabled me to dive deeply into and personalize my own healing journey. Sound has helped expand my intuition and my intuitive abilities and knowledge. I feel the sound waves create alignment in my cellular structure, and I do not have the appropriate words to share what that feels like. It's just a knowing, a feeling, a belief that I have.

For me, intuitive knowledge comes from trusting the nudge of our hearts. Listening to my gentle heart nudge opened up an entire avenue of life I couldn't have possibly created in my fear-based ego-mind. My ego held too many limitations, critical comments, and too much self-doubt. Connecting into my heart has balanced my belief in my worth and how I want being loved to feel. It has enhanced my ability to enter my relationships with my needs and boundaries intact. After sound healing, I have used that reflective time to clarify my relationship needs, how I want to enter them, and what I expect from them.

And I have been learning how to effectively express it all with love leading the way.

It's almost as if I felt the heart-nudge and tended to it like I would have a crying infant. I had to explore the discomfort and learn to eliminate what I could and to traverse what I couldn't. It taught me to let go of suffering caused by expectation. It's not like I have mastered it, but having experienced it, it seems easier to keep working towards being more kind with myself.

I was learning to love myself the way I so freely loved others.

The ripple effect expanded that, too. Now, I don't have a problem loving and honoring myself - because I am attuned to my heart. All of my work with sound baths and compassion have only increased the ability to show up that way for myself, too.

And my husband, the man I worried about, not supporting me? During a recent traveling sound session, he informed me that he loves being with me when I perform and that he's happy to be my roadie and biggest fan.

We have worked our way through some complicated things. These patterns in our relationship were 36 years old! Neither of us let go of our perspective easily, even though we both agreed that we didn't have a problem with change - we sure had a lot to work through! The work continues, and we jump in with our whole hearts. We're learning so much about life and love!

I love that dude, and I'm glad he rides the waves of healing with me as I progress through my exploration of sound. I sure believe the sound waves are having as much of a profound effect on his loving heart as it's had on mine. As well as each and every one of my clients.

Sayings:

"It is possible to find healing through Divine intervention. Our spiritual guides, and Angels respond when we ask for help. Healing oneself creates harmony within and better relationships are also created with others."
—Radhaa Nilia

MISTY PENNINGTON

ABOUT THE AUTHOR

Misty Pennington is an Alchemist, Master and Certified Usui/Holy Fire Reiki, and Karuna Reiki. Her modalities create transformative private or group sessions. She opened her healing space in St Peters, MO, in 2017.

She traveled around Missouri as a guest to yoga studios and meditation centers, sharing her Reiki and Sound vibration modality through Crystal Tones-Singing Bowls as a guide that supports her clients through harmonizing soundscapes into deep states of relaxation. As a compassionate healer, she successfully navigate the winding path of learning to love themselves unconditionally. It also helped her achieve a deep state of mental and physical well-being (moving out of anxiety) by focusing on her creative life while passionate about gardening and rituals that intersect celebrations on natural living.

Misty holds a Bachelor of Arts Degree in Human Resources, a lifelong student of the mystery of life, creating a safe space that helps her clients discover patterns that contribute to connection, harmony, and satisfaction in their ways of being. Before all this, Misty was a financial secretary at a public school district in 2015 and retired from a 32-year career.

Misty@Gardenofcommonground.com

7

HEALING ANCESTRAL LINEAGE
BY: MEREDITH RUBEN DANIELS

I grew up with a general belief that Heaven is where you go after you die. I believed my Grandma when she told me that Nene, my great grandmother who passed away when I was twelve, pushed a box sitting securely on a shelf onto my Grandma's head when she cleaned out Nene's closet. I can still hear Grandma's voice telling me, "She wagged her finger at me and said, 'Stop touching my things!'" I was comforted by the idea that we go somewhere nice when we die and that our loved ones are still there somehow, even sending us messages, but I never put deep thought into it or the fact that this communication could be a two-way street.

Later, I attended the University of Wisconsin-Madison to get a teaching degree, having wanted to be a kindergarten teacher my entire life. I was thrilled to do a teaching practicum in Sydney, Australia. I spent a month at Yeo Park Infants School, the cutest little schoolhouse in the middle of a park, and then my parents and my boyfriend (now husband), Kevin, came to join me so we could travel around Down Under for two weeks. It was an amazing trip.

On the day we were supposed to fly home, my Mom, Kevin, and I walked down to the post office to mail home a souvenir, while my Dad stayed behind to pack. When we returned from our errand about thirty minutes later, we knocked on the hotel room door for my Dad to let us in. There was no answer.

We banged on the door, yelling his name. Still, there was no answer.

Panicking, we went to the hotel lobby to get another room key. "When we unlocked the door, we found my Dad sitting on the couch, unresponsive." Paramedics were called, a heartbeat returned, and he was rushed to the hospital. The rest of us followed and spent agonizing hours in the waiting room while they worked on him. It was determined that my Dad suffered from a massive brain hemorrhage. There was no way for him to make it. We had to say goodbye.

My Dad immediately began sending us signs that he was still with us. Although he wouldn't want to admit it, my Dad was bald, had a round belly, and loved to eat (sorry for spilling the beans, Dad!). "While we were sitting in our hotel room a few days after he passed, a 'Simpsons' commercial came on TV." With his bald head and round belly, Homer was dressed as an angel, complete with a white robe and halo, digging into the buffet in Heaven. My Mom and I looked at each other in disbelief and laughed for the first time, saying, "I guess he found the buffet!" I watched for that commercial to replay the rest of our stay, but we never saw it again. This was just the beginning of the countless signs and messages he sent since his transition.

I spent the next several years trying to move on. The Universe was kind enough to grant me my lifelong dream of being a teacher, then promptly began showing me that it had other plans for me. I was incredibly frustrated because, after a few years, I knew that I wasn't supposed to be a classroom teacher, but I didn't know what I was supposed to be doing. I had spent my entire life training to be a teacher. I never tried my hand at anything else, and nothing else sounded like a good fit for me. During that time, Kevin and I got married and, a few years later, began our journey of having three beautiful boys.

I had grown up in a very Western medicine household. We went to the doctor, took our medicine, and never questioned anything. We never used anything alternative or natural because, frankly, it wasn't on our radar. I didn't even know those things existed.

When I was pregnant with my oldest, I had a realization that I was responsible for someone else's life now, and maybe I should change some habits. This led me to a Hypnobabies class, the beginning of the rabbit hole that introduced me to people who would greatly influence how I care for my family today. I had a beautiful birth, but I knew there was more to learn.

A year later, my doula introduced me to essential oils. This made a drastic change in my life, as I swapped toxic household products for natural ones and took charge of my family's health by using these powerful tools as our first line of defense. We all became significantly healthier. I was officially a "crunchy" mom.

Meanwhile, I was still trying to explore my relationship with my Dad. I knew he was still there, but part of me needed confirmation. I didn't want to hear it from a religious or spiritual person. I wanted a scientist with data to prove that there is, in fact, life after death and that all of the signs from my Dad weren't just in my imagination. I knew this was a tall order to fill, but I found the closest thing I possibly could to what I was looking for - "Evidence of the Afterlife: The Science of Near Death Experiences" by Dr. Jeffrey Long. In this book, Dr. Long discusses the hundreds of people he has studied who had near-death experiences. These people all had an experience where their hearts stopped, and their souls left their bodies, only to be revived. He interviewed people of all ages, religious backgrounds, and locations in the world. Their stories were all so incredibly similar that it couldn't possibly be a coincidence. I was sold.

From there, I went all in. Over the next several years, I saw healers, attended retreats, had readings with psychics and mediums, and became a Reiki Master. During my first session with a medium, several loved ones came through. Of course, my Dad showed up first, bringing me comfort around an issue I was having at the time. While he was the soul I most wanted to communicate with, to my surprise, Nene's message is the one that had the biggest impact on my life, and I still remember it to this day. She told me to take the path less walked on.

At the time, I had just returned to work from maternity leave. I knew I wasn't supposed to be in the classroom, and I was devastated to go back to work. Nene's message gave me the push I needed to explore other opportunities.

The next few years showed me the importance of personal development and introduced me to amazing, like-minded people. A friend told me about this amazing new technique she was trained in called GEM. It combined ancestral healing and essential oils, so of course, I wanted to try it!

At this point, I had just gotten my cycle back after having my youngest, and each month was pure torture. Naturally, this was the main issue we worked on. One GEM session later (this issue started with my youngest, so it wasn't as layered as many issues are), my cycles were barely noticeable and have stayed that way ever since. I was amazed and so incredibly grateful but didn't think to do anything else with it after that.

A few months later, I went with my mom to put her dog to sleep. As soon as she crossed over, a little thought bubble appeared in my mind's eye. I saw the dog as a puppy, jumping and saying, "Look at me! I don't need that old body anymore! I'm free! Yippee!" I was shocked and comforted at the same time.

Never having experienced anything like this before, I was baffled as to what it meant. Did I have a connection to the other side? Was I a medium? How do I have an experience like this again? A year later, I attended a medium development workshop and discovered that I do, indeed, have the gift to connect to souls who have crossed over.

While giving a reading, my client's grandmother came through. She told me that she and her Grandma both suffered from back pain and wondered if this was related. The first thing that popped into my mind was, yes, it was related, and she needed a GEM session. I knew that I needed to become certified in GEM to bring healing to the people sitting in front of me and all of the souls they bring with them. I became GEM certified that spring.

What is GEM?

Generational Emotional Mapping (GEM) is a type of ancestral healing developed by Joyce Turkington. Joyce was diagnosed with multiple sclerosis in the 1970s when Western medicine had nothing to offer her. Unwilling to submit to a wheelchair, Joyce began her journey to wellness with nutritional and dietary changes. After seeing some success, she dove into the world of homeopathy and saw further improvements to her health. Joyce then studied energy medicine, as well as epigenetics. After thousands of hours of energy testing, Joyce created GEM using a book of statements and affirmations. Years later, she was introduced to essential oils and realized that the oils could amplify the results of the GEM process. This led to the technique we have today.

GEM is based on Dr. Bruce Lipton's work with epigenetics. For decades or longer, we believed that we were slaves to our genes. If a family member had cancer, that automatically meant that we were doomed to repeat the same fate. In his book, "The Biology of Belief," Dr. Lipton states that we can have our genes express or not express a specific trait by changing two things, our toxin intake, and more importantly, our beliefs. If someone believes they will get cancer, they most likely will get cancer. If they believe they will be healthy, they most likely will be healthy.

The tricky part with this is that you hold your beliefs subconsciously. Simply saying "I am healthy" every day doesn't do much if you don't subconsciously believe it. There are different techniques to help you change your beliefs, such as hypnotherapy, but it doesn't end there.

The final piece of the puzzle is your ancestral history. When a person experiences trauma and buries or ignores it rather than processing it, that trauma becomes embedded in their DNA, as well as their energy field. It gets passed down generationally until someone heals it. Examples of trauma could be anything from abuse, rape, dis-ease, or loss, to a two-year-old getting separated from their mom at the grocery store. It's not the actual event that matters, but how the person handles their emotions around the event.

The emotions from traumas can show up in various ways - physical ailments, dis-ease, mental illness, behaviors, and limiting beliefs, and tend to get louder the further they get passed down. If you are reading this book, YOU were the one who agreed to heal your family trauma. You likely have had your physical, mental, or emotional struggles that led you to this healing journey, and you know that it is time. You have access to so many healing modalities just by holding this book, all things that weren't available to your ancestors. When you think about it, even one or two generations ago, society did not encourage people to talk about their feelings or go to therapy. Most people believed that life was hard for everyone, sacrifices needed to be made, and it's not worth talking about your pain because everybody has it. "It's better to suck it up and keep moving forward, no discussion necessary." Fortunately, that is no longer true. It is time for us to release the beliefs holding us back for hundreds of years so the collective of humanity can raise its vibration.

What does a GEM session look like?

We begin a GEM session by discussing the issues you would like to address. You are welcome to tell me as much or as little detail as you feel comfortable with. I am not a therapist or doctor and don't need the details, but I'm happy to listen if you want to share them. I then tap into your energy field and energy test to see which issue is the root issue to work on that day. While working on the root issue, the other issues will also improve.

From there, we find the origin of the misperception in your energy field that is causing your ailment. This includes when the misperception began, who it began with, and what factors contributed to it.

Next, we get into the oils. I test to see which essential oil you need and then identify which emotions related to that oil are stuck in your energy field. We see how many generations back those emotions go and which chakra to apply the oil to. If you don't have the oils with you, we set the intention that you have them. Then I read the "magic words" to you, including an affirmation specific to the oil used. The positive energy of the affirmation enters your energy field, neutralizing the negative emotions that were stuck there, and clearing them out. This allows your energy to realign, allowing your body to heal (physical ailments and illness almost always begin as emotions and energy first). We repeat this process until we have addressed this layer of your issue 100%. Most people call for a personalized essential oil blend to use after their session, which clears up any loose, energetic ends. I will test to see which oils you specifically need and mail your roller to you.

While some issues only need one session to clear up completely, many issues are like onions. They have layers. Each GEM session will address one layer in its entirety, but more sessions may be needed to clear the issue completely. I have no way of knowing in advance how many sessions a particular issue will take.

The truly amazing part of GEM is that it not only clears the issues for you, but it also clears them for every soul affected, going back to the original point of trauma, as well as clearing it for future generations. I often see my clients' loved ones cheering them on and expressing so much gratitude for doing this work on their behalf. I have seen chains being broken, bindings being cut, and people healing. It truly is an amazing experience! GEM is a beautiful gift to give yourself and your loved ones - the gift of healing.

MEREDITH RUBEN DANIELS

ABOUT THE AUTHOR

Meredith Ruben Daniels is a certified Generational Emotional
Mapping Ancestral Healer, Psychic Medium, Reiki Master, and
dōTERRA Wellness Advocate. Ever since she was a child,

Meredith felt called to help people. Her spiritual journey was prompted by the passing of her father, which led her to find the world of spirituality and energy healing. Her road was anything but straight, but Meredith is thrilled to have found her true calling in helping people connect to their loved ones and heal not only themselves but their entire family lineage. She is a firm believer that one person's healing helps heal the entire world.

Meredith resides in St. Louis, MO, with her husband (and high school sweetheart), Kevin, and their three boys. When not doing a GEM session, Meredith can be found sitting in a carpool line.

Linktree Link: linktr.ee/soulfulwellness

EVOLUTION OF CONSCIOUSNESS

BY: NEIL GAUR

Sound, Vibration & The Evolution of Consciousness

My name is Neil Gaur, and this is my story and journey of awakening and how it connected to my modality of energy healing. Firstly, to clarify what I mean by healing concerning my belief systems - I truly feel that we all have an innate ability to heal ourselves, and no one can heal you, especially when it comes to energy work and the realm of consciousness. If an individual is not ready to accept energy or the lessons in why they are out of alignment, then the 'healing' may not work. Even if the practitioner is so good at their modality, it has to be a mutual understanding and acceptance to take hold truly. My journey into energy work began with sound & frequency. Well, all things begin with sound since all things vibrate on the sub-atomic level, which I will get into a bit later. Ok, where to begin. Well, I guess the best place to begin is the beginning.

I was born in London, England, on November 17th, 1982. My

parents are from Punjab, India, but left for the UK early. I remember little about my early childhood, except for some traumatic experiences. Still, I remember feeling a bit disconnected or realizing that something was not right on the planet. The term 'right' is relative, in my eyes, since it can be argued that all things good and bad are meant to happen. I moved to California with my parents and sister at age 12 and continued my schooling there. At about 16, I wrote my first poem, and when I look back at this writing, I can see that there is a deep curiosity and desire to understand what it means to be human and why I was here on this planet. When I graduated high school and went to University, I was introduced to an entirely new world of music and people from all over. It created the situations I needed to ponder on life's biggest questions. I was raised Hindu but never truly believed in religion. I called myself an atheist Hindu because I did what I was told and didn't think about God. In college, thoughts would come to me as to the root of it all. Where did we come from, and is there a commonality to all these scriptures and religions in the world?

What is the root of all religions?

That one statement shaped the rest of my life. I quickly realized that so many religions all shared similar stories, that maybe there was an older story that they all came from. It made me ask myself the question, "if we know that these stories and myths all come from a common source, why do we focus on what divides us rather than our similarities?" This thought led me down the rabbit hole into intensive research on ancient scriptures, the possibility of Extraterrestrial life, and, yes, the modality I am here to speak on, sound, vibration, and frequency.

Being an Indian raised by a computer scientist and an accountant, I needed to understand concepts linearly before getting into the faith or belief. I found similarities in Hindu scriptures within Christian text, with Sumerian text, and so much more. These ancient scriptures spoke about sound and frequency and even travel from one dimension to another. It blew my mind. I realized that the Hindu scriptures had an advanced understanding of the quantum world and that by shifting our vibration, we can create harmony and reprogram our consciousness. This linear understanding of frequency is what brought me to spirituality.

The quantum world, energy, sound & frequency!

Humanity is at the beginning phase of understanding something that our ancestors knew all along. From 2000 - to 2008, I was immersed in rabbit hole exploration. Piecing it all together and exploring ancient wisdom, as well as figuring out who are the controllers of the world and how we got to this place of chaos, division, and duality. It was the time that was the precursor to my modality, which goes beyond sound (even though the sound is all that is) and includes a platform that I created which curates thousands of hours of presentations and works with many individuals who are all here to assist in the paradigm shift.

During this time, I was creating a lot of spoken word poetry. I have over 1,000 individual pieces. Many of them are designed to explore the nature of consciousness, ancient wisdom, and the universal questions of who we are and where we come from. I found it very easy to convey entire subjects in one poem. In 2008, I began performing my poetry at open mics, and this was also the year I had a dream to change my Facebook page name to Portal to Ascension. Portal to Ascension had been around for about two years, and I hosted a few sound healing events; however, in 2008, the name change went hand in hand with my shift from fear to an acceptance of the bigger picture and my mission on Earth.

Before I speak about my mission and the modality of creating mass content, I will speak about sound and vibration. We are vibrational beings, all in the physical Universe and beyond vibrates. Quantum physics is now proving that we are constantly vibrating frequencies on the sub-atomic level. Yet, we still see each other in physical form. Well, therein lies the illusion of this third dimension. Many ancient civilizations knew about this, and they created structures, tools, and scriptures with frequency in mind. When I first began creating events, I went on four tours up and down the west coast of the US from San Diego to Vancouver multiple times. Two of those tours were specifically sound healing event tours. Many of the tools we used were ancient instruments designed to align and harmonize our physical, emotional, and spiritual bodies. In these gatherings, individuals had incredible experiences and releases that allowed them to step more into their authentic selves and remember their beauty and divinity. It gave me a platform to create more awareness with vibration being at the foundation as I understood sound. We can speak of Extraterrestrials in relation to their frequencies, and even dimensions are various vibration levels. My modality of energy healing began with this and facilitating experiences for 1000s of people. It eventually morphed into presentations on this topic and beyond. We are energetic beings, and as we emanate frequency, all frequencies around us, within us, and beyond constantly affect our experience and perception. From the radiation of a star that supernovas millions of light-years away to the frequency of a friend you spend so much time with to the vibration of our planet. As we accept this truth, we begin to move toward a world of intentionality, balance, and true physical and spiritual healing.

The first few years of Portal to Ascension catered around sound and vibration and ancient awareness. Even the information-based events would begin with a sound healing experience. As I began to connect with more individuals worldwide, I incorporated many more topics and facilitated spiritual retreats, fairs, presentations, conferences, and workshops. The evolution and growth of Portal to Ascension continued, and I had a few milestone events that took us to the next octave. I would be traveling from city to city for years, sharing the awareness that I acquired and working with so many luminaries. It was hard work, and it honestly did not pay the bills. I often decided to quit and work a corporate job until this past milestone. In 2015, I shifted Portal to Ascension into an online university of conscious exploration. The live events continued, but I began facilitating an online conference every month on a different topic. It quickly became a full-time job, and the same year I quit my corporate job and never looked back. We went from one event a month to 4 a month within a matter of a couple of years, and at this point, Portal to Ascension creates and hosts over 110 conferences, webinars, and tours a year. Live events, online webinars, and taking authors on tours worldwide to share their messages. I remember at one point I was wondering how to show all the diverse experiences I facilitate on my website. Now we are at that point, and I am honored to have worked with over 1,500 presenters, researchers, yogis, spiritualists, scientists, consciousness explorers, and more and created well over 2,500 individual events. Our archive has over 10,000 hours of conscious awareness, and I am fully embodying my mission to assist in the Ascension and assist others who have dedicated their lives to this 'work.'

It has been the most satisfying and rewarding experience of my life to do what I do. Sometimes I wake up and remind myself how incredible it is not to lose sight of the opportunity to serve and live my passion full time. It has been a long journey that includes hardships, challenges, and joy. As Portal to Ascension evolves, so do I, and my inner healing is an ongoing process as I understand who I am and bring light to the traumas I have faced. It is only just the beginning, and what we have in store for the years and decades to come will continue to impact this planet and all life on it in a positive and transformative way.

NEIL GAUR

ABOUT THE AUTHOR

Neil Gaur is the Founder of Portal to Ascension, a conscious event production company created in 2008 that hosts a wide range of presenters on various topics such as the origins of humanity, the existence of Extraterrestrial life, exposing hidden truths, and exploring the nature of reality. He travels the world with his wife Sol, facilitating gatherings and filming documentaries to empower individuals to reclaim their sovereignty and awaken to their full potential. Neil also operates an online platform that creates and facilitates about 110 conferences and workshops a year. At this point, Portal to Ascension has worked with over 1500 researchers, spiritualists, scientists, consciousness explorers, and more. Neil is a philosopher, historian, researcher, and spoken word artist. He presents his research on the ancient wisdom and future science of sound, vibration & frequency, and in-depth explorations into ancient civilizations, archaeological discoveries, space anomalies, shedding light on hidden esoteric wisdom and exploring ways to create unity and peace on Earth. www.PortalToAscension.org.

9

MADE OF STARDUST

BY: EVA VENNARI

I was on the treadmill, the kids were getting ready for school, and today's mistakes hadn't yet come to pass. As clear as day, while looking at the wall in front of me, the face of my x-lover appeared. I hadn't spoken to him in a few years, and I hadn't thought of him other than in reference to "things that don't work out."

Why now?

Brushing this vision from my mind, I shifted to other ideas like tasks for my day, how long have I been on this treadmill, wondering why walking for this long only equates to 90 calories burned. Deciding to be done, I hopped into the shower. Within moments, I started to sob. The tears were sudden and not my own, meaning I wasn't feeling sad.

When I asked myself, "Why am I crying?" I heard the clairaudient reply, "Call him."

Call him! "Who?"

My x-lover's face appeared in my mind's eye once again.

"Nope! That's not going to happen. He cheated on me and married someone else."

The sobbing became extensively worse. There was no controlling it. My eyes were blurred, and I was wracked with an emotional pain that doubled me over. It did not stop for as long as I was stubborn.

Relief only came with my reluctance, "Fine."

Finishing my shower, drying off, and making my way over to my phone couldn't happen swiftly enough for whoever was guiding this action to call.

Picking up my phone, I turned it over, navigated to dial, and stared at the screen in disbelief. Now, I deleted his contact information from my cell phone when I found out he was only playing with me those years ago, and now all I needed to do was hit SEND. His number was there on the screen.

I'm not going to worry about the how at this moment... and I hit SEND.

I'll never forget the two and a half rings before I heard a weak voice, "Hello?" It was him. "Did I wake you?" I asked with a slight surprise.

He started to cry, "No. I live in Texas, I'm married, and my wife just died."

She ended her life, and he found her laying on the floor in their bedroom. He had been giving her CPR while in grief and hysteria. That was the pain I felt while in the shower.

"How did you know to call?" he asked.

"I felt you."

It was the beginning of a discovery of what's yet to come!

Experiences come to me through those I am metaphysically connected to in my life, those who experience heightened emotions of either bliss or pain. Spirit asks me to take action.

I do know the why, though. I remember metaphorically

raising my hand to be a part of something greater than myself, to be in service, in whatever way I could. In hindsight, I can see this experience as a training ground for learning to trust.

A year later, he was remarried, and not to me, again. We remained friendly, honoring the connection. We're on the phone, and he shares the trouble he's having with the house. He's moving back to his hometown but can't seem to sell that house in Texas.

My experience is almost automatic. When someone starts to speak on things that bother them, I follow what feels like an electrical impulse down a metaphysical wire to that thing, and I can read its energy. I digress.

In this instance, as he's speaking about how he can't seem to sell the house, about how many people are attracted to it, take the tour, but find themselves disinterested once they reach the master bedroom, I said,

"Could it be because of what happened there?" I asked him.

"What do you mean?" He replied.

"It doesn't occur to you that suicide could leave an energetic mark on a physical place?" I digress again.

Immediately, my clairvoyance kicks in, and I see the room in the house as if it's a cake and someone has cut it in half to reveal the layers. I see the upstairs bedroom, and where there's supposed to be a floor is a black hole.

I shared with him what I could see and offered as gently as possible the concept of "what she's left behind," it makes offers on the house impossible!

While he was considering that, I asked, "Do you want me to see if I can do something to clear the energy?"

I'm more than 1000 miles away physically, but I know this doesn't matter. By now, I'd learned whatever I needed to do to help clean up energy that could be done in the ethers. The ethers have no address. It saves a ton of gas.

He commenced a monolog that started with a "Yes." That's all I needed. Permission is everything in the world of healing. I tuned out his voice and got to work. By the time he was done with his reasoning, I had plugged the black hole and repaired the energetic floor of the bedroom so that it had the same resonance as a new baby's bottom.

"It's done. You'll have an offer on the house within a week," I announced.

And he did. He waited a week after that to call and tell me, but I knew anyway.

These became regular events for me in time. All my channels of intuition were slowly and steadily coming online, being refined, and allowing for these very private but profound healings. There wasn't anything that turned them all on. I've always known I was different, but something was keeping me "between stations" like an old TV that's not quite bringing in the picture clearly. Static.

So, what was causing the static? Well, I could fill an entire book talking about how we choose convenience over substance as human beings. We diminish our "antenna" of awareness from food choices to ignoring our intuition. You can call this a story of awakening if you like. But my real focus is on making that antenna better than ideal.

Around the same time, I sought medical attention for roughly 30+ different symptoms my body was offering. I had a barrage of issues ranging all over the place: Chronic Fatigue, anxiety, insomnia, itchy skin, short-term memory loss, fibromyalgia, arthritis, heart palpitations, hypothyroidism, known toxin measures, and more.

I used to tell my doctors, "I feel burned out," which is now an actual medical term (you're welcome). But I was laughed at back then.

My favorite way to describe my low blood pressure was to tell friends, "I'm 98 over dead."

The vertigo was so bad at times, and it would happen while I was driving.

I ended up with degeneration of the L4-5 in my spine from who knows what? In my 20's, this kept me in so much pain that it would take a good five minutes to fully straighten up upon standing. I lived in chronic pain for well over 16 years.

When I sought medical attention, the doctor who analyzed my spinal MRI said, "You'll be in a wheelchair by the age of 35, here's a prescription for depression."

I fired him.

By definition, the daily migraines weren't migraines because medicine dictates you can't experience them daily. But they had all the other signs of a migraine. Eventually, nothing brought relief. That doctor who analyzed my MRI said that if I continued down this path, I'd be on Social Security Disability and depend on the government for my livelihood.

I believe in being a productive part of society. Remember, I raised my hand to be in service. That wasn't going to work.

10 fired doctors later, I found myself being "blessed with insomnia" at 3 o'clock in the morning, plugging in all my symptoms to a Google search. After many links followed, I found an article describing what it would feel like to live in a body that had been depleted with minerals.

The lists of symptoms I was living with were all there. I found myself in this story, and the solution fits in with my desire to not take drugs. More importantly, it reflected my belief that if you give your body what it needs, it can heal itself. I had found the world of Mineral Balancing with hair analysis.

Mind you, I had a doctor perform hair analysis with me years before. It turns out you can read a hair test incorrectly and make a person worse. That is what happened then. Turning to the ones who created the process and offered educated analysis seemed to be the difference. I decided to give it another try.

• Within a few weeks, I cleared the grief of my grandmother, who had died seven years previously.

• In a month, my chronic muscle pain had diminished to rare occasions.

• For the first time, I experienced a normal menstrual cycle after nine months and reversed my perimenopause and infertility.

• My chronic migraines were finally gone.

I've forgotten most of my chronic symptoms now, and it has nothing to do with short-term memory loss. They are now independent things of the past. I live without them in my experience.

How? We are made of stardust. No matter how you look at it, our bodies are part of the Earth, and she lives amongst the stars. Our bodies are our temples. It's our temporary home and must be cared for, or it will prematurely age.

That brings me to my next story.

Seeing such wonderful results with Mineral Balancing, I decided to become certified in the process. I wanted to take advantage of the perks being a practitioner and be in the position to help friends and family. It was only a very small light somewhere in consciousness that said, "Maybe you could do this for a living."

Two weeks after being certified, I find myself on the phone with my x-husband. We had been divorced for 12 years by then, and we had just finished sorting through family details about the kids when he started to share his physical woes. For many years he lived a life of excess. He was a professional rodeo cowboy and abused himself hard. Now, he was experiencing several symptoms, including Hep-C, heart prolapse, gird, bloating (looked pregnant), recently diagnosed with type two diabetes, and now the doctors were telling him he had iron toxicity. These are all signs of chronic imbalance, and many of these symptoms can be eased if not eradicated using mineral balancing.

"Why don't you send me some of your hair, and we'll get you sorted?" I offered. He laughed, "No, no. My doctors have me. I'm on medication."

He experienced a massive heart attack during a procedure to remove kidney stones. He was taking 17 medications. Two weeks later, at the age of 45, he was dead.

That prompted me to open my business which later became The Elevate Institute. What happened next was so outrageous I hid it from the world until I could no longer.

After my x-husband passed away, I kept receiving a clairaudient message that I knew wasn't regular spirit vernacular. It was "cowboy." It was my x! Instead of moving on, he attached himself to me. It was a true problem!

Seeking help, I attended a metaphysical fair that just happened to be during my next day off. There I found someone calling herself a "psychic surgeon." There was a conversation around my experiences and what she felt was the right course of action.

"Fine," we began.

I was introduced to etheric places, and energetic guidance I never knew could exist. Sure, I knew angels from being raised Catholic, but this was a different level.

We were now in the Contract Room, and we were there together. I described what I saw. To both our surprise, she could concur and see what I saw from her own perspective. She hadn't ever experienced a client who could "see" with her before. We were discovering something about me.

The contracts between my x-husband and I were read, marked as complete, and given to the soldier angel to throw them into the fire. It was time for my ex to leave.

The angel turns to me and says, "Now it's time to clean off his soul body and send him to the other side."

"You're the angel! Why don't you do it?

I am still a bit lippy to this day...

"Because you're the human," he explained.

This was a profound moment. For all the moments we're waiting for otherworldly forces to step in on our behalf, I realized we fail to acknowledge that we have untapped power within us for healing if we just ask for guidance.

Being human is where true co-creation between Universe and self lies.

I allowed for the training, learned the tools necessary to clean a soul body, create the light – the portal to Heaven itself, and help a sentient soul mate with the transition. My psychic surgeon told me that my auric field was brighter and no longer compromised by my ex.

Cool.

Over the years, I continued cleaning my body of the "static." Mineral balancing safely removes toxins easily. It's part of what I call the 4-stages of healing. Through displacement, minerals take their rightful place in the body, which is the catalyst for what everyone calls detox. It automatically releases medical drugs thought to have exited the body already...nope. That stuff is stored in hidden places. The beautiful thing about relieving yourself of the toxins is that the side-effect lifts up the immune system. All those viruses like Epstein-Barr, Scarlet Fever, and other forms of strep I took antibiotics for weren't killed off. They remained in my body for years, causing inflammation hampering my immune system. When the immune system works better, it's amazing what it can fight.

My experience had gone from that of great frustration, thinking I had a bum body to a profound sense of faith in my body's ability to hold my spirit, not just live, but thrive. It wasn't broken. I just didn't know what it needed.

After more than a decade of healing myself and thousands of others worldwide, I see the results in this work. Combining Mineral Balancing with my spiritual gifts has opened the freeways of the mind for greater emotional processing, clearing of old wounds, clearer thought, and more energy for bringing in each person's unique gifts.

~

Sayings:

"Healers do the invisible work of cleaning this world up, one wound at a time."

—Radhaa

EVA VENNARI

ABOUT THE AUTHOR

Eva Vennari is on a mission to dismantle the status quo of the sickness industry. Having spent most of her adult life suffering from all kinds of conditions and fighting for her sanity, she decided to take matters into her own hands. That's when everything shifted, and her body went from being the enemy to being her best and most devoted ally and partner.

If you're full of "static," you're unable to connect clearly with Source. It is each person's sovereign duty to understand our soul's contract. In not doing so, you deny the rest of us your gifts. Getting in touch with those gifts and having a profound positive effect on our fellow humans is part of the journey of healing when you work with The Elevate Institute. I invite you to elevate yourself.

Website link: https://www.theelevateinstitute.com

10

FALLING IN LOVE WITH DEATH
BY: ERIC RAINES

Death is the ultimate fear in this life of ours. The unknown, the specter of ending.

When alone at night, when fears creep in, thoughts often turn to the space of our mortality and how one day, we will have no choice but to cross that bridge, just like every single person who has come before us, who set the stage for us. The curators of then, as we are the curators of now.

It has led to untold amounts of anxiety and fear throughout human history. This fear has led to untold levels of suffering for Humanity and dropped the ball right in our lap. Today. Now.

There are many levels to the fear of death. The fear of being left alive after all your loved ones are no longer here, the fear of stepping into the unknown and not knowing. The fear of watching someone gripped by that ancient process as they struggle to stay here. The fear of wasting away until death seems like the prudent choice.

In my experience, fear has always led to the path of the highest good, if studied, if transmuted and if explored.

It has created an understanding of death that is not a piece of common knowledge but has provided me with comfort, joy, and Love in facing my death.

I had a near-death experience (NDE) in 2014 that completely revolutionized my life. I stepped onto the other side of that experience, invigorated and full of joy, full of Love for life and death.

As I was convinced that I was dying, I felt a split or a physical sensation of being here, and very distinctively, on the other side of that split was the complete unknown. I felt my body shutting down and the split getting stronger. The unknown grew with intensity, becoming the only thing I could feel with certainty as my body grew more and more numb--dead.

I knew that I was on my way through, and a terrible fear gripped me. I was dying. As I lost touch with my body, the fear seemed to fade away, as if my body were the only thing able to feel fear, but I was left with what only felt like me. The I AM.

Inside of this sensation, I realized something that changed my life forever. If I must die, why would I go kicking and screaming? Why would I step into something we all have to do with fear? Do I like being afraid? Of course not, so what is the purpose of stepping into the unknown shaking and terrified?

It seemed completely nonsensical to me. So, I smiled. As I stared through the veil, I felt myself becoming excited and happy. It wasn't the end. It was a brand new beginning. A space for me to explore the truly unknown in a way that was impossible for me in my body. And I made peace with my death. I truly welcomed it, and all fear forever dissolved.

You see, death is the reason we fear. It is an ingrained psychological and physical response hardwired into our nervous systems. We fear not having enough shelter because it leads to us dying. We fear not being safe because danger means we can lose our lives.

Every fear response eventually leads back to death.

So, if we transmute that fear into joy and Love, suddenly there is nothing to be afraid of in our lives. There are most definitely things we do not prefer and do not align with, but even that can be experienced with Love and joy, transmuting what is not preferred into a clean, open space where we can build what we DO prefer, what we DO Love.

This NDE happened between two major events in my life.

The Deaths of my Grandmothers. My Grandmother on my father's side was the best Grandma any kid could have wished for. Loving to a fault, supportive in every way, and the best excuse I could ever have to eat a ridiculous amount of candy.

When she was dying, she was so scared. She made sure that she would be resuscitated every time she flat-lined over the space of 3 years. She refused to sign the DNR (Do Not Resuscitate) order and demanded that they bring her back every time. Over three years, it destroyed her. She was in so much pain and so tired that at the end, she told the doctors that she just wanted to go home. She couldn't do it anymore.

We got her 24/7 in-home hospice care, and she died listening to her favorite movie, Gone With the Wind, surrounded by family.

It was hard for me. I was terrified of living MY life without MY Grandma. I never considered her fear. I never took into account her pain. When she died, all I could think of was me and how much I hurt.

I never once told her that I supported her and that it was OK for her to go. She wasn't just terrified of dying; she was terrified of leaving her family behind. I never really got over her death until I faced it myself.

My second Grandmother on my mother's side was one of the sweetest people you had ever met. Very proper and punctual, always ready to teach what was right. We would listen to Bobby Derrin and Nat King Cole together when I was a child. She was the reason I was able to go to private schools until high school, something I never realized until I was an adult.

She died four years after my NDE, and the difference between the two was staggering. She was just as scared as my first Grandmother, but she had more spaces of clarity where she could process and understand instead of just feeling fear and weariness.

When I went to see her for the last time, I couldn't help but relive my first Grandmother's death as we drove down. The difference in my reactions was profound. I hadn't paid much attention to it until I was forced to go through it again. I realized that I wasn't going for me this time. I was going for her and her alone.

I would love her and help her feel joy inside of such a terrifying space.

When I walked into the room and sat on her bed, I reached out and touched her face. Her eyes opened, and she focused on me.

"Eric?! Oh my goodness is that you?!"

"I love you Grandma. You were the greatest Grandmother I could have ever asked for, thank you so much for loving me like you did."

"I love you too Eric...I am scared. I don't...I don't know what to do."

"I know. It's OK though. We all have to do it and I will see you again as soon as I step through that door to come meet you. You don't have to be scared. You don't have to worry about us. We are strong. We are smart. And we Love you so much."

These words were sparked by how I felt. The last thing I want is to see my beautiful Grandmother in pain and scared. I was here to help transmute. I was here to help her transition. And it worked. I became a focal point for her to let go truly.

As we are dying, we lose touch with what the body feels. We go back into the senses of the Soul. And she felt me. She felt that knowing that the Love I have for her death, my death--death in general, comforted her. My joy--the permission she felt not to be here for us soothed her in a way that words cannot quite describe.

She let go. She stepped out of fear and comforted the rest of the family before her passing. She was lucid for another few minutes as the rest of my family said their goodbyes, and there was nothing but excitement and Love in that lucidity.

She died four days later, but that was her body. That was not her.

As I write these words, I feel both of my Grandmothers with me. So full of Love, so full of support.

These three events have shaped my life in a way I never expected. Such beautiful examples of the extremes I felt and the journey that had shaped my path into this space.

I became a Death Doula for my Grandmother. Like a Birth Doula helps bring a new human into the world. I helped her passing be as pleasant as it could be as she left.

It is the energy I write about. "The Energy of Life." Death just so happens to be a part of life. It is not the evil monster hiding in the shadows. It is truly an old friend coming to walk us home. It is a testament to who we are in how we react to it.

It is the proving grounds.

It shows us who we are.

I invite the world to become a Doula of Death, for themselves, for their loved ones, for the world in general.

Transmuting this fear will lay the Foundations of a magnificent existence for all of Humanity and transform your world into something incomprehensible.

Death is Love. It is our choice whether or not we react to it with fear.

From my heart to yours,

Eric

ERIC RAINES

ABOUT THE AUTHOR

After a Dark Night of the Soul culminating in 2012, an intense energetic activation in 2013, Eric Raines became aware of the implantation and parasitic construct by direct observation. His subsequent search for answers about this experience led him on a journey to self-discovery. This discovery, coupled with more and more real-world practice, has allowed him to gain a deep understanding of how this invasive system works, how to identify the interferences and constructs, how to promote self-protection through daily practices, and, most importantly, how to remove these false constructs from himself as well as others.

Constantly expanding his repertoire of tools, Eric currently implements various energetic tools ranging from parasite/implant removal, meridian clearing and balancing, crystalline organ rejuvenation, GoldenTheta healing, soul fragment retrieval, remote lymphatic work, and Golden Light energy work. He also utilizes physical based practices such as Quantum Pause Breathing, Reverse Breathing, Self lymphatic massage, Cycle Stretching, Chi Kung (Qigong), and meditation. He is an ardent advocate of aiding the entire human race to achieve their full, natural potential.

As a receiver of this hidden esoteric knowledge, Eric considers it his duty, his life's purpose, to share this information with the world, to free all of humanity from the ravages of this system, and to help create a world filled with Love and light, and Unleashing Natural Humanity was born!

https://www.unleashingnaturalhumanity.com

11

40 LAYERS OF THE AURA
BY: ANNEMIEK DOUW MSC

D o you ever realize that you are a Soul in a human jacket? A spark of Light, a divine expression of consciousness that has chosen to have an experience here on Earth?

Yet you are. To have the perfect experience, you made a plan in advance. Depending on its purpose, the plan contained the ideal parents, a certain place of residence in a particular country and town, the skin tone you needed during this stay on Earth, the date of birth on which the journey began, and a date on which it will end. Everything relevant for a successful voyage of discovery on Earth was chosen. During this process, you also made agreements: Soul Agreements, contracts with other Souls that could assist you during your stay. Disguised as lovers, business partners, children, friends, and sometimes also as people who'll give you hard times. They all help you experience exactly what you chose yourself as a Soul before you embark on your journey.

Your Soul Plan describes all these Soul Agreements and other desired life events. And once a Soul has landed in a human body, you can find the blueprint of all these plans for its current journey in its aura.

Aura Layers

The human aura is the energy field that surrounds you; it's your personal space. It consists of several energy clouds that increase in size. Your physical body is the smallest and densest cloud, and around and through it are several larger ones, fields of energy, each of which is bigger than the previous one. The difference between two consecutive fields is called an aura layer. Every field has its vibration and consequently holds a different frequency, the energy of which relates to a unique life theme. Within this energy field, your aura, you find information about who you are, your present life goals, and how you've processed past experiences so far. There are also indications of what you planned further along the road and with whom. All you wish to do, it's all there.

By experiencing and processing life events, you develop consciousness and grow as a person and a Soul. But sometimes, those experiences aren't easy, and you temporarily forget that you are a radiant Soul in a small human jacket. This is when you think that earthly reality is real. Then you're less connected to the Light within, and you're a little less aware. You lose the higher perspective.

When you get caught up in the daily drama of life, something clots in your aura, resulting in choosing other things for yourself than those that are good for you or what you want on a Soul level. It changes the course of your life.

A trauma causes this; a hurt. Wounded on a physical, emotional, psychological, or spiritual level. Traumas often express themselves physically because you can only feel what is bothering you in your body. But that does not mean that the origin of your problem is also rooted here: sometimes it's in your aura, in your energy field. Then you need to heal the level and theme that you didn't completely process.

Practice

Since 1998, I have worked with thousands of people, clients of all ages, in the private sphere and within the business world, and the questions, problems, and illnesses that people come to me with vary widely: Why do I always fall for the wrong men? My child sees ghosts and is afraid of them. I am not recovering from the enormous fatigue and the chemo I received for my breast cancer. I want to get pregnant, but I can't. I have cancer / MS / CFS/ ABI. Can you help me recover and heal? I no longer know which choices to make in my life or work. I have major problems with my family. Can you help?

All these cases have one thing in common: I help by looking into the aura layers concerned, giving words to what is going on, and energetically repairing the trauma using the healing energy from my hands. This is called 'spiritual surgery.'

What Came Before

Surgery is a far cry from my original career choice. Trained as an engineer, I used to live 'inside my head.' Before the big turnaround came, I worked as a manager in the corporate world. My brain was the ship captain, and I almost had a burnout because I worked too hard and didn't listen to my body anymore. That body was sending signals, but I skillfully ignored it. And so I got stuck and needed to do bodywork to reconnect with it again.

Doing this, I discovered I was clairsentient. I not only felt my own pains and emotions, but I also felt in my body what was happening in someone else's.

To learn to deal with this properly, I went back to study and learned, among other things, the secrets of working with the aura. I turned out to be clairknowing, clairaudient, and clair-voyant as well. Psychic in many ways, reading energies, trans-lating them into information, and healing them, I learned to see the future and talk to the dead. My world keeps getting broadened...

I started my practice and lived a wonderful, healthy life. Nevertheless, I still fell seriously ill a few years later. Doctors couldn't help and these years taught me that illness wasn't necessarily the result of doing something wrong - something that I had learned during my studies, and it wasn't a judgment of your body. No, during this Dark Night of the Soul, I found out that sometimes it means that you did something 'wrong' and sometimes it doesn't.

Sometimes you get the flu, for example, because you haven't taken enough rest. But at other times, you develop a condition because you had previously intended to go through this as an experience on Earth. Then it's part of your Soul Plan.

40 Aura Layers

When I discovered this other way of thinking, I finally could heal myself and return to work. Being ill, I'd learned to speak and work alongside guides, deceased loved ones, and all kinds of Light Beings. Working again, it also turned out I suddenly noticed more aura layers than the seven that I had learned about before.

Intrigued by this, I decided to investigate them. If seven life themes are presented in the first seven layers, which would emerge from the others, I observed? What could be the route and meaning of life?

Of course, I wanted other people to benefit from the discoveries I made so they could heal (themselves) and go through life more easily as well. That is why, after years of working with them, I wrote my books about the 40 aura layers, the 40 Layers of the Soul.

A Diseased Friend

Finn was lying on my treatment table because his best friend had passed away a few months earlier, 46 years young. He didn't believe in my work as a medium, but he wanted to try it anyway.

I heard his deceased friend say: "Do you believe in this hocus pocus?' and I thought: That isn't very nice to say about my work!' before repeating his words aloud. Finn immediately sat up with eyes like saucers. He had goosebumps all over and was sure that I had his friend on the line because, as it turned out, they had been in a band together for over 30 years, since the age of 16. And the first song they ever wrote was called Hocus Pocus. For Finn, the proof was provided. I treated the wound in aura layer 21, which contained his energetic wound. Its theme was recognizing and connecting with the Soul in every human being, looking past the human façade. Finn quickly calmed down while we talked with his friend.

When I later tried to make notes in his file, I suddenly hesitated writing 'hocus pocus,' and I wanted to write it with a K. Finn smiled and told me they called their song Hokus Pokus. That made it so confusing.

Crybaby

3-month-old Anna came to my practice with her 4-year-old brother and mother. She was a crybaby who had cried non-stop since birth. Even now, she cried heartbreakingly. I noticed a lot of tension in aura layer 12: family themes. In 12, you're connected with your partner, ancestors, parents, siblings, and children. Family in all shapes and sizes: biological, step-, foster, and those unrelated, but feel like family.

As she lay on my treatment table with her mother on one side and me on the other, I discovered that she was suffering from the tension between her parents. They were on the brink of divorce when they ended up in bed one last time. An unplanned pregnancy was the result. But, because of the new daughter's arrival, the spouses decided to stay together, resulting in many quarrels and fights. Anna couldn't deal with the intense energy and expressed this by crying.

When I completed working in her aura, she immediately became quiet and started to smile for the first time in her life. It was such a beautiful moment. A happy mother in my practice, a smiling baby on her arm. Now the mother almost cried out of sheer happiness because this had never happened before.

Her brother then asked if he could also lay on the table. Since they shared the same traumatic energy in the family layer as they were part of the same family, I agreed. I just started working, when instantly his little sister started crying again! Everyone was in shock; had the problem not been solved completely?

Then I realized that she was probably reacting to the changing energy in her brother's twelfth aura layer. Since this layer was connected to hers, she presumably was uncomfortable with the energy change. When I was almost done healing the brother, I said: 'I'll count backward from 3, and then I feel she'll be quiet once more.' I tied off the aura and began the countdown. '3, 2,1.' I stopped working, and it was as if I had pressed a remote control. The baby became silent again!

This is how you see that family members are connected in aura layer 12 and respond to each other's energy on that level. So, it's not only about what is said out loud; it's about always being connected, even if you no longer see each other and have officially broken contact.

A Seven-year-old with a Death Wish

A 7-year-old boy who no longer wished to live came to my practice. His parents were, of course, deeply concerned. I saw him in a previous life, in which he had died at the age of seven. He didn't realize that it was a different life in this life. He listened to that old song. As it were, he read an old road map. One stopped at seven, so he now had no idea what could come next, making him think he didn't want to go any further. I fixed the error in his programming, and after that, he could move ahead, living according to his current Soul Plan.

Relationship Pain

Hardly anyone likes the termination of a relationship, but sometimes it seems nearly impossible to get over it. In these cases, the one left behind feels a gaping hole and misses out on several life events that can't occur simply because the partner they would be experienced with is unfortunately lacking. Then there is usually a Soul Agreement that is not or only partially fulfilled.

The aura layers this trauma is presented in impact your life. For example, if it is in layer 34, 34 consecutive layers and themes are touched. They're all affected by the grief over the relationship that ended prematurely. This way, the violated Soul Agreement negatively affects your life and choices on several levels. Repairing the wounds enables you to heal, recover, and choose freely again, no longer burdened by the past. As a result, new

Soul Agreements can be made, and happier times can be created.

Tinnitus or HSP

People experiencing tinnitus and Highly Sensitive People both suffer from problems with the nervous system. Often, they present with hick-ups in aura layer 18, the perfect place to learn to deal with duality. People with tinnitus tend to neglect to listen to their bodies. And HSPs, on the other hand, listen a little too well and usually are quick to withdraw from the world because they cannot deal with the diversity and quantity of stimuli it provides. In both cases, the solution in aura layer 18 is learning how to use your body as an instrument, picking up the message, and then letting go of the energy on time. Of course, themes in other aura layers can also play a role. In this case, in layer 18, it's either about learning to listen in time (tinnitus) or retreating too soon as a means of protection (HSP). It's about learning how to energetically take care of yourself and recuperate if you've become over-stimulated.

Your Aura or Your Life

Fortunately, if things don't work in life and your aura gets clotted, you can do something about it. You can approach this in two ways: if you learn to deal with things differently or process what has happened and heal a certain part of yourself, your aura changes on the corresponding level. Vice versa, if you heal your aura at the right level, your life (and your health) will change accordingly.

Sometimes you do this healing work yourself, and sometimes you might need a little help. Then the universe has a beautiful way of assisting you by bringing the right people and solutions to your door. This works through resonance and the law of attraction. You attract situations that invite you to encounter and resolve your issues since you are like a mini cell tower. This way, your request is often answered without consciously asking for it.

Help Yourself

So now, if you have a problem, you can start helping yourself by using the 40 aura layers. Please visit   https://www. annemiekdouw.com/free-tool/ and look at the aura picture; it contains all basic healing energies, like a vitamin bomb. Just align with your Soul and connect to the tool. Tune into its energy and see what resonates within. It may well be that this gentle trigger helps you heal sufficiently.

Your path

If you need more healing, please get in touch with me or one of the other solutions the universe provides you with. And please rely on the self-healing powers of your body and trust your Soul as a compass for life, as it remembers what you came to experience. If you combine common sense with the supporting resources that the universe provides for you, your life can be healthy, joyful, and fulfilling. And you will harvest what potentially was already there, and that is the plan of your Soul.

Sayings:

"Being patient with the healing process as the wound pain comes to the surface may get worse before it gets better. But this is what it takes to heal and it's all part of the healing journey. So never stop. Keep on healing your wounds."

—**Radhaa Nilia**

ANNEMIEK DOUW MSC

ABOUT THE AUTHOR

Annemiek Douw MSc (1966) is a Dutch healer, medium, management coach, trainer, and author. Her background in engineering, her studies, and her work as a healer, combined with her personal experience with long-term illness, has led her to understand how to heal at a Soul level. Her USP is healing in the 40 layers of the aura. She shared her unprecedented work in the books: 21 Layers of the Soul, Healing the Karmic Ties with Friends, Lovers, Family and Enemies (2013), 40 Layers of the Soul revealed (2015, in Dutch), and her self-help book The 40 Senses, the High way to a fulfilling life (2020, in Dutch). Annemiek helps people heal at the 40 levels of the Soul. She teaches them how to use their own Soul Compass and heal themselves and others. She works both in-person and remotely, in English and in Dutch.

Find Annemiek at: https://www.annemiekdouw.com/free-tool/

12

I AM THE UNIVERSE

BY: MARIE UNIVERSE

I am the Universe, four of the most profound words I have ever spoken. Therefore I decided my healer name should be Marie Universe. I also felt like my guides helped me choose this name.

I had developed postpartum depression after my son Neiko was born and was trying different medications from my doctor to help. None of them helped me. Over the years, pain in my body and stress started getting to me from working so much and not taking enough time for myself.

Finding myself in the darkest place, I have ever been and becoming suicidal made me turn to spirituality. I wanted to go into a more natural route when my doctors couldn't find a solution and none of the pharmaceuticals would work. I turned to plant medicine, yoga, a vegan diet, and meditation.

I started using Cannabis and CBD oil regularly. Cannabis is my spirit plant and has gotten me through all the hard times. Spirituality gave me hope, inspired me, and saved my life.

I also developed what I believe to be fibromyalgia and

Raynaud's syndrome. I also had carpal tunnel, extreme back pain, and muscle cramps. I knew my diet had to change., I knew I had to change. I would plead for help on the causes of my pain to my doctors. They were never any help. I started to take my health into my own hands. I started manifesting a healthy mind, body, and Soul. I started doing yoga. I started to eat less meat. I rewired my brain's pathways to be more positive. I always wanted to go Vegan, but somehow, I could not leave meat completely. I remembered coming across information on Plant medicine and wanted to use it for healing and grow my relationship with my higher self and the Universe. I would never have imagined they would have such a significant impact on my life.

Psychedelics can heal addiction, anxiety, depression, and PSTD. I was excited to give them a try. I remember seeing a video about a man who gave up his alcohol addiction with micro-dosing LSD. He says that he thought to himself "how he should stop drinking, and he never had the desire to do it again while on LSD." He just knew his relationship with alcohol was over, and I think that is powerful. Psychedelics had come into my life during powerful times when I needed them the most. They always say that "Psychedelics will find you when you're ready," and I believe in this 100%. I was shown the Magick and love of the Universe, which still amazes me today. In 2017 I had my first LSD trip experience, and it was otherworldly. I was immersed in the present moment and this blooming reality of love and light.

I felt no pain in my body, no sadness. I just felt a pure connection to all that is. It was a music festival, and I had just "dropped the acid." It started storming. In my mind, I felt like I could attract a lightning bolt. Well, then the next crazy thing happened. Lightning struck our campground, shocking some of us. I still remember the jolt of electricity that shot through my body as I held our poles into place so the wind wouldn't blow our campground down. As the storm let up, I started to peak. I remember I started getting visualizations. My entire reality started spiraling like I was watching Dr. Strange. During this powerful trip, I had the same experience I had seen talked about online, breaking addiction with psychedelics. I had, which at the time was a profound thought, "I don't want to eat meat anymore." At that moment, it was a powerful realization that I had power over what I ate and that I didn't have to eat meat again. It's like there were no mental barriers. I was free of self-doubt. It helped me overcome my addiction to meat with just one dose. I've been Vegan since May 2017.

"Veganism, meditation, plant medicine, and yoga had led me to a place with no pain."

I was beaming. I was also seeing angels' numbers off the charts. My lucky number especially started popping up everywhere. I saw 777. It made me feel so good to know I was aligned with The Universe. I was micro-dosing Psychedelic mushrooms "Golden Teachers." My awareness and consciousness were thriving. I had cured my panic attacks with the help of DMT, Cannabis, and Golden Teachers. I remember I started having Magickal occurrences. I saw signs everywhere that I was a healer. My psychic abilities, as well as manifesting abilities, were as strong as ever. I remember the first-time healing someone was when my cousin had trouble with her Thyroid. She was almost in a fatal condition. She had a very stiff neck and pain from it. After we hung out, I felt like I took some of her pain on after I sent healing. I felt my neck Stiff, and it was hard to even sleep with the pain. But it quickly went away the next day. She started to feel better, and I haven't heard anything of the condition since.

Kundalini Awakening

In March 2019, I remember getting home from work, and I felt so tired, so I thought to just lay my head down on my desk for a few moments. A few moments turned into hours. Suddenly I sprang up from my chair. I started feeling these jolts of energy moving through my body. I could not stop my body from shaking. It was the most powerful thing I had ever felt. I was feeling full-body orgasms from the Universe. I could barely mutter the words "oh my god." I fell to the ground and could not control the movements of my body. Then it felt like pure white light was pouring into my chest, and I was almost levitating off the ground. The only thing keeping me on the ground was my awareness. That night, I was having visions and out-of-body experiences. Sleeping was like meditation. I felt Gods and Goddesses, higher powers, visit me. I felt like Kali represented herself to me. It represented this profound change in my life. My mom had come to check on me, and she knew I was not myself. I was acting very strange to her. Of course, I was acting strange. This Kundalini awakening had awoken my psychic abilities and turned a bit into what is known as a "Bipolar Awakening." I was skipping up and down my mother's street and talking to my guides. I was jumping for joy; I was able to hear them. My mom was not excited. She did not understand it. She sent me to a local mental hospital. I had the worst time in this hospital and tried to tell them I was having an awakening. They did not understand it or even try to. They forced me on pharmaceutical drugs. I had a terrible time alone in that hospital without my pendulum, crystals, or comfort. I felt as though I was being spiritually attacked, left and right. I was able to read minds and send thoughts. I was in a higher state of mind permanently. You hear of the Buddhist monks who can reach these states of consciousness, but we think, is this even possible in myself? Psychedelics truly are the training wheels. I have been "tripping" ever since my Kundalini awakening. Hearing your guides and tapping into these Clairvoyant powers is a Western world nightmare. I remember standing in the mental hospital, and they were all coming through at once. I told them quite literally, "Shut the Fuck up!!" I literally could not hear myself think. I also wanted to avoid a schizophrenic diagnosis by the doctors, so I didn't want to be talking to myself. My guides understood because then it got quiet. The main theme from my kundalini awakening is that I have Healing abilities. I knew this was possible because there I was, healing myself.

I gave in to the doctors and took their medicine because, at that point, I just wanted to be out of the hospital for my son. I don't remember the first two weeks in that hospital. I remember the first couple of days. I remember I was healing everyone around me. I was feeling energy very sensitively. I kept passing out and still having shoots of orgasms through my body. I remember one of the nurses thought I was acting. They had a fall risk band on me. I had a cup of water at one point, I was almost done drinking it, and I noticed a hair at the bottom of the cup. I took it to the nurse. After I told her about the hair in the cup, I heard, "Well, if there is a hair in the cup, why don't you just throw it." I believe this was the thought that I was hearing from the nurse. It sounded like her voice. Strange enough, when thoughts come through from others, I hear them in their voice. So, I just did it, tossed my cup, and it tapped her foot. She told me that was assault and then proceeded to lock me in a room alone. In my defense, I was a bit out of it; I hadn't slept in days.

The kundalini energy can be dangerous, I hear. It will cause mania and insomnia. I remember feeling so claustrophobic and having to use the restroom. I was pounding on the door to use the restroom, and they would not help me or let me out to use the restroom. I remember peeing in the corner of my room twice. Then they came into my room. I told them I didn't want any medicine.

I would have complied if they had told me what they had to do. I remember smiling and being in a blissful state. Then, there I was, laying on my stomach. Suddenly, about four nurses started holding me down, and they jabbed multiple syringes full of medications into me. I started crying for help, yet the security officers in the room just looked the other way. I had bruises from where they jabbed me, and I couldn't sit down on my rear end without pain for weeks. I blacked out after they gave me the medicine. I have no clue what happened next. I do remember, however, meeting many people like me in the hospital, people with spiritual powers that are being masked as "Mental Illnesses." When I got out, life was pretty normal. Except it wasn't, I had just had the most profound experience of my life. I knew I was a Healer and had these extraordinary abilities. I wanted to contact the media. I wanted any help I could find. I wanted to help and be the change we need to see in the World.

After getting out of that hospital, I had a "Dark Night of the Soul." I felt as if I was attacked by Black Magick in that place. I felt them try to take my Prana away from me. The sad part is they succeeded. This was the most heart-wrenching feeling one can have. Imagine being fully connected to the divine, feeling blissful and full of love. Then it's just TAKEN AWAY. I still remember the black pit I felt in my Soul. Like nothing was there. I couldn't feel the energy. I felt devastated. But Dark nights of the Soul don't last forever, fortunately.

It has been very humbling being a channel for the Universe. To spread healing and love is my main goal. It made my heart so happy when a client reported feeling love again after years!! Another one of my client's children had many food aversions. She was a very picky eater. I sent a clearing for this, and immediately her daughter asked for noodles. Her mother was stunned and relieved. I've also had a healer tell me I gave his higher self one of the most powerful healings he has ever had. He was originally connecting with me to give me an Attunement. Yet my higher self had other plans. My higher self had healed him of his fear of speaking. Some of his stuttering symptoms were relieved! I thank the Universe every day for this beautiful life and the ability to channel energy and transmute it into something beautiful.

There's just so much to talk about. I'm excited beyond words to keep having profound spiritual experiences and working for the Universe. I always receive a deeper understanding of myself and the World. In return, I get to help spread this knowledge. Even though I have had the roughest spiritual path, I am thankful for it, every single part. The Universe and God are always right on time. I want to share a very intimate moment with God and The Universe. One day last year, in 2021, I took my son to school. I had been behind on orders in my shop. I was feeling very overwhelmed being a single parent and sole proprietor. I walked him to school sobbing a bit because I did not want my son to be late again. I had to get more organized. I began to feel the lightest refreshing, beautiful rain.

The Universe always sends me rain when I need a cleanse. I said to the Universe, "Is this rain for me?' Then I got a confirmation... the rain getting slightly harder and the wind slightly more dramatic. I started crying a bit. Thankful to the Universe for healing, safety, and comfort. I asked the Universe again. Is this rain really for me? "Then stop it," I said in my mind. The rain completely stopped. I was stunned and in awe as I looked up at the sky. I said, okay, now, "start again." And it started raining so hard, the wind had so much pressure. This overwhelming sign of the Universe talking back made me cry the ugliest happy tears I had cried in a while. I am in awe at the Universe every day. You are always heard when talking to the Universe.

I feel very blessed to know who I am and what my Soul's purpose on this planet is. I have felt like I was chosen by the Universe to go on a special mission. I hold the fire that will burn this pernicious system to the ground, only so that a new one may bloom ever so beautifully. New Earth is here, and we are here to assist Gaia in moving to the next evolutionary step in consciousness. Using, Oneness, Love, and Magick are the three ingredients needed to create a better world for our children. You are the Universe experiencing itself. Remember that.

BRITTANY MARIE FOUCHE, AKA MARIE UNIVERSE

ABOUT THE AUTHOR

Marie Universe is a creative entrepreneur who has had various Spiritual Awakenings. She was Senior class president and graduated 4th in her class with high honors.

Marie Universe is a Psychic Medium, Healer, Spiritual Life Coach, Herbalist, Universal Mystique, and more. She has had profound Spiritual experiences that she believes will help her change the World! She has helped them overcome Subconscious blocks, emotional triggers, and more. She has over two years of Energy Healing experience and has already helped 1,000 people worldwide through her Etsy store with over 500 five-star reviews. Just like many other Starseeds who have come to Earth with the same mission, she is simply honored to be here on this planet during this glorious time of healing, transformation, and ascension.

You can reach Marie at: Etsy.com/shop/marieuniverseloves

13

WHEN A PILOT FALLS DOWN
BY: AMY THAIN JORGENSEN

When A Pilot Falls Down The Rabbit Hole

Scrolling through social media posts, the title of a book catches my attention. It has been three years since my only daughter passed away, and I am still struggling with grief. The title is something to do with "releasing" past emotional trauma. Seems interesting, although I have looked briefly at things like this in the past. All this "woohoo" energy stuff like Chakras and whatnot. None of it seemed aligned with what I was taught in my previous college studies or my religious culture, and certainly not in traditional therapy.

For some reason, on this day, I was able to put my doubts off to the side more than I had before. I started looking into "how" exactly people were trying to justify that they could work with a person's "energy" as part of a way to help them feel better.

Let me take you back a little bit further. Coming out of college, I joined the Air Force. My husband at the time had become a stay-at-home dad. Seemed like a perfect little scenario.

We left our little hometown feeling like heroes. Making something of our life felt adventurous!

When you are focused on a career, it can be hard to recognize what is happening in your own family. A couple of things began to transpire. I was in and out of my home, deploying, attending training, and I thought everything was great. However, my youngest child was not coping with my constant "coming and going," I didn't see it. I had a second issue beginning to fester. I was dealing with my own anxiety. I actually hated flying, but here I was, on this pedestal. There was no way that I was going to admit that. It was a physically and emotionally draining secret to deal with every day.

A new assignment had sent us on another move to California. While we were settling in, we decided to leave to run it to town for dinner. My anxiety broke, and what started as small cracks in the wall burst open into an unmanageable emotional flood. My 8 yr old son was putting on his socks. He suddenly snapped, overwhelmed with not being able to get the "seam" just right. He ran up the wooden staircase, locking himself in his room. He began yelling, threatening to jump from the two-story window into the boulders landscaping the house below. The move was too much for him to process. I crumbled as I looked at my husband, who unemotionally told me this was normal behavior. My heart cracks open, and I immediately call a psychologist.

I had been gone so much that I had no idea that my own child was suffering from some detachment issues. After having him evaluated by multiple professionals, it was apparent that he needed some serious intervention. This broke my own anxiety thread, and I had a mental breakdown. Newsflash, the military is not keen on letting you walk away after spending 1.5 million dollars training you. I felt completely helpless.

I moved my family back to Idaho while desperately trying to get out of my commitment. At least there, we could start working on a "stable" life, and we had family that could help to care for my son emotionally. I was unsuccessful. For 6 months, I lived alone in an empty apartment, figuring out how to get back to my family. I finally found a path to the Utah Air National Guard. It was a two-hour one-way drive, but this was progress.

I began taking on little jobs here and there. We had lost our full income, and Shane seemed really "comfy" being from home. We had also started a small dehydrated food mix business, and Shane began running it full-time from home.

The color of a red flag is brilliant when we are looking pack at our past. Shane did not adjust back to "civilian" life. We were financially struggling, and our business was insufficient to support our family. Shane could have written his own book titled "When your toxic father burns your dreams."

Shane had always planned on taking over his family's irrigation business; oddly enough, you could actually see it from the front door of our new house. His father had been in and out of jail and had a little issue with some addictions. Before we had left for the military, Shane ran the business full-time.

I remember exactly where I was standing in the room, we had turned into our "commercial kitchen" for our business. Shane looked at me with excitement. His dad was going to sell him the business. I wanted to follow in his excitement, but this was not the first time this had been promised. A few days later, his dad unwound his offer just as before. Shane was devastated and slowly began to fall into a deep depression.

Concerned about how Shane was acting, we started couples therapy. We separated but continued living in the same home, "our little secret." I had started training again and was only home on the weekends. Once again, I had no idea what was happening in my home, only this time, the mental health issue was with my husband and not my son.

Shane ended up leaving one afternoon, and he never came back. How did this happen? I was 34 years old with two boys, ages 10 and 13. Rumors began to soar, and I lost the support of my church group, but some of my own family members became heavily involved in gossip, sabotaging my life. People did not realize their fangs were affecting me, but my children had to be removed from school when their friends began "repeating" what they heard in their homes.

I fell quickly into a relationship with Dave. We had an instant connection. He was also recently widowed. We had grown up within houses of each other. At the time, he was one of the only people I felt understood what I was going through without judgment. Emotionally I became completely "numb." I learned quickly that two damaged people don't equal a healthy relationship.

I had to get away from my little town. I grew up in a strict religious community. You don't live together before being married. Surrounded by our parents and children, we got married in a local church one random afternoon. At least I wouldn't have people judging me for "shacking up," and I was able to move into Dave's house, putting some distance between myself and the small-town gossip. Dave became obsessively controlling. Our relationship reflected his past issues, and he began isolating me from everyone else. I was punished emotionally for talking to my own children.

I was so lost that my life became a daily fight to want to survive. Behind the closed doors of our house, I was paying a heavy price emotionally. I had already lost everything I had. I was in survival mode, trying to make my marriage work. Where would I go? How could I try to start again? I was in the cyclic trap that can only be understood by someone in a relationship with a narcissist. Dave loved me, and he was always sorry, and I was always accepting, hoping somehow his words would be true this time.

We added another child to our family, a boy. He was a joy to us, healing some of my heartbreak. In our previous marriages, we could not have more children, so this seemed like a light of hope for me amidst our unhealthy relationship. Hoping for a daughter, I became pregnant 10 times, and I continually lost the baby between 4 to 15 weeks with each pregnancy. This added to my emotional numbness. We decided to stop trying, and the next day I found out I was pregnant. I began spotting, expecting the same scenario. I was far enough along that we went in for an ultrasound. This time there was still a heartbeat!

At our scheduled 20 week appointment, we heard the words that we thought were impossible. We were having a girl! Both of us were in shock as the technician continued with the ultrasound. I started feeling like something was wrong. This was taking too long. The technician left the room, and the Dr appeared with words that shattered the only piece of my soul I had left. She could see a defect in our daughter's heart. "You will have to see a specialist. I cannot tell you any details about what I am seeing."

The following months were hell, to put it mildly. Being pregnant with a baby you know has a health issue that can't be assessed until after birth is a mental prison. I learned to hate the words "everything will be okay." I learned this lesson once before, that phrase is a lie.

Kyndlee was born and passed away 26 days later. I lived in a camper, 2 hours away from Dave and my children, while I watched her battle. The separation escalated Dave's narcissism, and I watched my daughter fight for her life while I mentally fought for my own.

The day of her funeral was my breaking point. I was either going to take my life or change my life. The words of another directed me on the path of changing my life. Intervention from above happens like that, a certain person at a certain place saying something that clicks with your soul. I had made an appointment at the request of my OB, who could see through my fake face that I was in deep depression. She sent me to my family practitioner, who took the time to "actually" talk to me. His words, "focus on yourself, get to your place of happiness on your terms without worrying about what anyone else is doing."

That was it, so simple yet so difficult. I stopped putting pressure on myself to "look" for the perfect part I had always managed, set my boundaries with Dave, released myself from the stressful religious mold I had learned, and began to see things for myself.

There I was. Looking back at everything I had lost, my career as a pilot, my first husband, my only daughter, and myself. I had no purpose, passion, or path, and I did not like how it felt. All of this directed me to my cocoon, where I was growing a beautiful set of wings inside. What looked like a complete mess was actually part of something beautiful.

I came across the book, let go of the chains from my religious-tribal beliefs, and began absorbing as much information as I could get my hands on -- related to energy work. Miracles began to happen, first for me and then for others.

My past healing became my passion. After working on my own wounds, I began helping others witness this same process for themselves. Client after client, I began to see miracles happening.

My first "wow" moment happened during a session while

working on my first certification. I was doing another session on another healer. At first, this was intimidating to me. Still, using what I had learned about clearing away negative beliefs, I could release this barrier for myself, and working with another practitioner was suddenly no longer a source of anxiety.

This practitioner wanted to focus on what was causing her an issue with her ability to work on herself and others. I began to "see" an object. At the time, I did not realize this was the beginning of my realization that I could channel images, objects, words, people, smells, and all kinds of things as communication for myself and my clients.

The image was in a tube, about the size of your hand. As I looked closer, I could see it was a tube of toothpaste. This made no sense to me. I said, "there was some kind of energy issue around a tube of toothpaste." She knew exactly what it was.

Her sister had just lost her son in a tragic accident. After the accident, the sister came to my client's house to stay for a few days while making all the necessary arrangements for her son's passing. The sister had left her toothpaste in the bathroom, and my client had started using it. The energy from her sister's emotional trauma was being transferred from the toothpaste to my client! I told her to immediately remove the toothpaste from her home. A new phase began for me, "you can't make this stuff up!"

This phrase occurs daily for me now, client after client. I continue to see things, smell things, and hear things. It is so incredible. The blessings this work brings to others fill each moment of my day with overwhelming gratitude.

My past has now become my purpose, my passion. This beautiful unfolding manifests itself with new connections and new opportunities every day, one of those being the birth of ELV. Elevate Life Vibration is an energy healing methodology channeled to me after hours and hours of studying and working with clients.

The focus of the ELV program is bringing traditional cognitive therapy practices together with the energy healing practice of releasing blocks from the subconscious. By combining the two approaches, I found that amazing changes happened for my clients, bringing relief from their physical pain, reduction in their symptoms, and an overall feeling of balance in their lives.

I have a philosophy that healing and finding joy and balance in life should be accessible to everyone. The more we raise our vibration as a whole, the more we come together at a higher level of consciousness, and beautiful things happen for everyone! Part of my purpose is to continue creating resources that are easily accessible to others. In addition to offering remote healing sessions one on one, courses, and a certified practitioner opportunity, I offer free weekly training on my Blocked Emotions social media platforms.

I can't wait to see you bloom into your beautiful soul-centered self as you become part of this vibrational energy shift.

AMY THAIN JORGENSEN

ABOUT THE AUTHOR

Amy is a true example of how life can give you everything, then take it all away!

Once an aspiring military pilot, she had it all when suddenly her husband lost his life to suicide, leaving her a single mother. Three years later, she lost her only daughter to a heart defect.

Amy completely fell down the rabbit hole, she had lost all

hope, self-confidence, and her inner fire from previous accomplishments smoldered away. With divine intervention, she was led to energy healing. After fully embracing the beautiful practice of releasing past traumas, Amy developed her own methodology for trauma recovery, and Elevate Life Vibration was born.

Amy now uses her past struggles to heal as her purpose, fulfilling her passion by bringing joy and smiles back to those who have been burdened by physical, mental, or emotional obstacles. She offers this through individual sessions, courses, and a certified practitioner program.

You can reach Amy at: BlockedEmotions.com

14

HEAVEN ON EARTH WITH ASHTAR

BY: LALITAH SUNRA

I was born for these times. And I am pretty sure that you were too.

We are in the dawn of the Golden Age, and now more than ever, we are needed: the healers, the sensitives, the empaths, the Starseeds. We are here to create the New Earth.

I never felt I fit in anywhere, not really. I felt I was on edge looking out at people, trying to fit in, and understanding their behavior for most of my childhood. I didn't understand why the grown-ups said one thing when it was clear to me that something else was going on.

I sought something that made sense to me and explained my existence here. I searched high and low - in psychology, philosophy, astrology, etc., to find more meaning. Did others feel the same way that I did?

As a young teenager, I remember perceiving my dead grandfather coming to visit us, checking in on us, once in a while. It was a source of solace and pleasure to know he was still around.

I also had very clear visions on how we could live peacefully and harmoniously on Earth from the heart - though I could not articulate it in this way back then. It all got tucked away in the very back of my memory for a long time. Mostly because it did not fit into the 'norm.' I had strange reactions when sharing my thoughts and experiences. Both the otherworldly visits and my visions of a peaceful life on Earth. It even frightened a few people. And others started arguing politics with me.

I didn't have the experience of feeling heard or received with the things I shared, so I stopped talking about it. Instead, I did what most people in my shoes do: I adapted or tried to. I adapted my way of speaking, of presenting myself, of arguing. And I guess I became quite good at it.

But a part of me was missing, and the void it created led me to seek in other ways, and hence I entered the alcohol and weed smoking period of my youth. There I at least found some fellow rebellious spirits and other misfits, and I could enjoy some escape for a while. The weed helped me escape into my fantasy world and connect with some of the parts that I felt I had lost. It also gave me a distance from the 3D reality I was living in. The alcohol gave me the illusion of having fun even without my lost part, and I could forget my frustrations and exhaustion from all the efforts to fit in. It required so much energy to keep that other part of me hidden all the time! The alcohol provided only temporary courage. But at what costs?! It didn't bring about any solution or ease in my daily life.

It wasn't until my late 20s/early 30s that spirit, life, the universe, or whatever you want to call it, nudged me in a different direction. The nudge came in different ways to me:

• Sudden moments of clarity when I knew I had to stop using alcohol the way I was doing.

• Moments of realizing the emptiness of some of my relationships.

• The awareness that love was something quite different than what I'd thought it was.

But the most obvious sign of all was the buzzing in my hands, which suddenly started from nowhere, right in the palms of my hands. I couldn't compare it with anything I'd felt before: A warm fuzzy feeling that was accompanied by a strong sense of peace and a feeling of connection to a bigger intelligence. At moments it seemed to take over my mind and body. I felt protected and calm whenever it showed up.

In the same period, I started having intense migraines for the first time.

These experiences led me into the world of healing and energy medicine. I had to find out what was going on with me.

But how?

Then one autumn day, when I was lying in my bathtub, my eyes fell on the local newspaper saying that there was a big Holistic fair in a venue just a 5-minute walk from my apartment. My hands started buzzing, so I knew I had to go. Perhaps I will find my answer there.

So after my bath, I snuck out of the house since I was supposed to go to a board meeting in our building. But this felt more urgent.

When I arrived, I saw a palm reader and thought to myself, "She must know what is going on with my hands," so I signed up for her 5 PM slot.

When the time came, words suddenly blurted out of my mouth. "I don't think it is my turn!" I said. A bit surprised, she replied, "but it is 5 o'clock".

"Yes I know it is, but I don't think it's my turn!" At that moment, two ladies came, and it turned out they were ahead of me on the list. I figured it would be too late for me to have my reading by when they finished. But I had no idea what else to search for there. So, a bit disoriented and disappointed, I walked around looking at the different stands. I then found myself attracted to a reiki stand. I was reading the brochure when a woman from the stand approached me, saying, "why don't you just jump up on the bench and try instead?"

⌐ Two minutes later, I found myself lying on a massage table in a big hall with two women putting their hands on different places of my body. It all was very silent, and I didn't feel much until the buzzing started up in my hands again. Soon, 'my body was lulled' into this peaceful but strong energy.

By the end of the session, my body was vibrating, and I was feeling good. I asked one of the women if she knew what the buzzing in my hands was about. She looked at me deeply for a short while and announced, "But you are a healer!"

I was both surprised and not surprised. While I had read something about healing in my quest to understand what was going on with me, I still didn't get it. What was I supposed to do with it?

In reply to my question, she advised me to learn to use the energy and to master it, so I could decide when to activate it and when to turn it off.

She referred me to a reiki teacher, and I signed up immediately after I got home. Reiki means universal energy – and that is what I learned to work with. That became a life-changing shift for me. Working with the energies felt like coming home. Here my inner world made sense. I had found my path, and suddenly I had hook into life.

It turned out it wasn't that simple in the beginning to combine this newly discovered world with the world I was living in. There was skepticism among those around me, and since this world of energy was my safe space, I didn't feel like sharing it with people who didn't understand. But slowly, I began to give sessions, pursued more training, and even got myself a small clinic and gallery in Copenhagen. Ever since stepping on this path, the energy has evolved and taught me more and more about my depths and life. It has become my leading star. But still, I felt like searching and didn't fully find my place.

It is no secret that we have had a tough time the last few years. I remember the very first lockdown. I was surprised by the inner joy I felt: the joy of having more silence in the world and knowing that this shift in times is what I came here for. It was so evident that my abilities had been gifted to me for something bigger, supporting this shift of the Earth.

We are now seeing the old ways crumble and no longer survive. We are seeing truth being exposed, as well as shadows and non-truth, we are clearing and purging, and at the same time, we are rising. The Earth is Ascending, and I came here to assist in this shift.

Shortly before the lockdown, I began to channel Ashtar, a Galactic entity involved in keeping peace in our Galaxy. It was very new to me. I had never had anything to do with the Galactic before, and I was surprised because my rational self had avoided it. But yet again, it came to me by itself, and it felt like home.

I read about the Central Sun and found that besides having a physical Central Sun in the Pleiadian star system is the activator and creator of our Solar system, the Central sun is a portal, a state of consciousness where we realize ourselves as creators and connect with our Goddess/God essence and create Heaven on Earth. So Ashtar gave me Galactic Shaman, Central Sun, and a symbol that I understand represents the Central Sun. He showed me how to use the symbol he had given me as the base for my healing modality, which has changed a lot since I first learned Reiki. And he told me that we would receive spiritual technologies that our minds couldn't comprehend yet.

Now, as I write, I understand that I was given a new healing modality, and it reaffirms the joy and clarity of purpose. I KNOW why I came here. I am doing this healing work to awaken people to their God/Goddess essence to become the New Earth Leaders to create Heaven on Earth.

The method helps to clear all that is not you and assists you in coming back to your essence by igniting the light in your cells and opening your heart to allow that bigger to flow through you. It activates your Soul codes and your crystalline DNA. And I know more is to come. And for me, it is so exciting to know that now is the time. I feel honored to be working for the universe in this way and grateful for finally feeling there is the purpose to my being here. It is what keeps me going when I see all the craziness and fear being released around me.

Since Ashtar first came to me, he has been with my partner and me a lot. He is always there to help upgrade and mentor me, even without being very direct. I also learned that he is connected to Andromeda, another Galaxy, where we live in 12D consciousness and Oneness and don't understand our division on Earth. People say he comes from the Pleiades, but that is a station for operating in our Galaxy. I learned that I originate from Andromeda, which explains why I struggled to understand and feel ok in the game of the 3D Earth.

Well, I could keep on sharing, but I thought you might want to hear from Ashtar, so I asked him to speak to you who are reading this book.

What Ashtar shared:

"Be greeted Beloveds,
I am Ashtar, the Commander. I come and go in peace.
I am observing the Earth from a bigger perspective. We have placed a light grid around your planet. It is there to illuminate your brains and your cells. To re-activate the light within you. As the light re-activates, you will see the "monsters" that have been hiding in the shadows. That is truly happening now for the Earth and you individually. "
Ashtar continued.
"Many of you who read this will be connected and directly tapped into this light grid. You will know what I am talking about. You are activating your medicine and bringing it to play just as it was meant to be.
We want you to know that it makes a difference AND that the light is strong. More and more are being touched by it day by day, and you are doing your part to spread it.
We are very excited about the opportunity to speak here and bring light to you all through the written word. Isn't humanity exciting?! You have so many ways to spread your light and to communicate it. We wish for you all to find yours. We communicate through energy and sometimes through mediums, like now, here. Energy is our main way.
That is why some cannot yet see or sense our presence because they are not in touch with the feelings of subtle energies. But it will be the language of your future; it is where you are heading, and we are here to make it happen and to awaken those cellular memories in you. Your capacity is immense, just like ours.
We brought you a gift. A simple method to stay awake and clear the way to receive the energies we communicate. To stay in your center and keep your pineal gland clear. This method will help you

activate your pineal gland to illuminate your brain so its capacity can expand.

We encourage you to use this method to tap into the light grid around the Earth. As of now, it is strong. It is like a plasma of light, and we keep an eye on it. It is the fastest and simplest way to affect people. More of you will rise, more of you will wake up. You will begin to sense another way. You will find your values in life, you will experience things from a new level, and you will continue to evolve. We are excited to support this ascension and to collaborate with you. We are excited to reach you. We want to encourage you and imprint a light grid in your mind. We wish for you to see and understand the currents of change around you, even when they are invisible to your eyes.

That is why we encourage you to clear your pineal gland to see with your third eye. The eye of bigger truth and perspective.

We love you all

We love you all

We love you all

I am Ashtar – together with the galactic federation and Andromedan peace council. At your service.

We come and go in peace."

In Lak'esh"

You can get your Blue Breath Exercise here: http:// mysteryschool.centralsun.earth/blue-breath-ashtar-subscription/.

~

LALITAH SUNRA

ABOUT THE AUTHOR

Lalitah is a high-frequency Soul Activator and is teaching soul technology with the guidance of Ashtar. She has been working professionally in Energy Medicine, Tantra, and creativity since 2007. She is internationally inspired, comes from Denmark, and resides in Turkey.

All that she teaches, she has practiced herself. She is authentic and walks her talk. She is connected to the 5D realm, which allows her to see things and perspectives not everyone sees or understands.

Since she surrendered to following her soul, she met her life partner, moved country, opened more and more to her multidimensional abilities, and created and lived her dream life day by day.

Connect Lalitah here: https://linktr.ee/Lalitahsunra.

15

SACRED RELATIONSHIP ALCHEMY
BY: STASIA BLISS

I had done everything my reality had told me I should do to live happily ever after. And yet, it was all wrong. I felt all wrong. My new marriage was stale and even harmful to my newly blossoming womanhood. My mate didn't know how to please me, and I didn't know what it meant to be pleased. Something deep down inside me urged for the "perfect union," as I think we all do, the bliss that might somehow be touched through merging with another, but I was far from understanding what that was or how to get there at age 21.

It took two marriages, a few serious spinal injuries, including a head-on collision that should have killed me, and several trips around the world to study in India before I was making the connections between awareness of my life force and how to manage it - and the relationships and intimate experiences I was having and longing to have.

In India, I was blessed to study with an incredible Tantric Master who taught me much and transmitted even more in the ways of life-force and union. I came to understand that Tantra -

though very misunderstood in the West - means "to liberate" or "to free" one's mind/perspective; To know God in all things, and to understand that there is not a thing that cannot become a pathway to remembering who we truly are. This understanding alone dramatically transformed my life and how I saw my relationships, including those I would have deemed "toxic" or not right if I'd followed societal rules and definitions. Suddenly, I was free to find joy and meaning in every relationship rather than calling them failures when they would end.

My Tantric teacher would constantly repeat phrases like: "it is already happening, you don't have to do it - just allow it to be" or "just feel it, it is already happening" and" feel that you are being moved rather than moving your body." These ideas and sensations stuck with me -at the same time, they unstuck me from thinking I had to be doing all of this - because I could tell it wasn't me who was enacting this soul-awakening I was undergoing. I mean, yes, it was me getting up at sunrise to do the exercises, and it was me staying until high noon doing them, but I was only putting myself in front of the process - which is what I love to tell my clients. It was me who was agreeing to experience something more - by simply showing up. It was my "Yes" - in other words, that made it so.

Boy, oh boy, in that time on the beach with Sahm doing Kundalini exercises daily, and I'm not talking Yogi Bhajan style. Still, ecstatic yoga - mind-bending universal awareness - the most incredible divine sexual portal opened for me during that time. The two men who were practicing with me, one of whom was my boyfriend. The life force energy we were navigating together was so open-hearted and sensual at the same time. We felt so close to each other and so vulnerably exposed that there wasn't anything we could do to more deeply revealing ourselves to each other save to make love and share the love that we made.

Before those moments, I never imagined two men could be so generous and kind with each other and the woman they were both enjoying and honoring. I felt like the ultimate goddess being taken care of in a pure field of love, ecstasy, and openness. There was no judgment or rivalry, just presence, and bliss. At least until "reality" hit us all - a space/time bubble that we each had to learn to navigate in our ways.

I suppose you could say I've had a most colorful life full of experiences that most people only read about or imagine, and I have loved many and enjoyed many more. Through those experiences and the deep intimate understanding I was having about my own body and the spiritual mechanics, I uncovered what I'd consider the mysteries of sexuality and relationship and the revelation of inner alchemy and what relationship alchemy means.

Following the threesome in India, I returned home to find my life-force energy supercharged. What was previously "just fine with me, was now not expansive enough," so the exploration continued. Each encounter I have had has shown me another facet of the potency of love, desire, sexual union, and the things that occur between two people's energy bodies. I found myself strangely both the discoverer and the keeper of some very deep and beautiful love secrets. Some of it was wonderful and lovely. Some of it was frightening and had me facing deep fears and concerns about myself and life. In all cases, I was engaged in what would best allow me to integrate my wholeness and then teach that to other people.

Through the opportunity to know love with another woman, I also learned a new perspective of love and being loved. I experienced what a man might feel trying to pleasure, love, or support me, which softened me to men even more. I started to fall in love with all the facets of man - and therefore, my rendezvous and love affair with her - will forever be a magical key I know helped me unlock the unconditional love I wanted to know with and for a man.

When two people come together in intimate union, they enact an alchemical field of transformation that cannot be avoided or stopped. This is happening with the person you are with right now, though most do not realize it. This understanding alone is pivotal in transforming relationships on the planet and, therefore, the evolution of love. If we do not know that our relationships are catalysts for transformation, and we do not understand how that plays out in the body, then it is very hard to find beauty in the hard times. It's even harder to wade through the alchemical fires without running away.

At this time, I believe the world is in dire need of the information I have been embodying and teaching for years. This includes an understanding of the sheer holiness of our beingness and the honor it truly is to witness the awakening process in another person - and to be simultaneously witnessed - for that is what is going on unbeknownst to most.

The healing I have received in my body and my relationships comes from the beautiful understanding of the body-mind complex as a perfect vehicle of the evolutionary process. That truly we are divine beings incarnate, here to remember who we truly are and shift our dimensional awareness, so to speak, in the way we relate, love, and experience pleasure.

It is my opinion and wildish life-work to know that each of us is capable of a divine interrelating that we might only have imagined belonging to gods and goddesses. Though it is also my opinion that this, we are. We have reached a crescendo in our human evolution that demands that we see relationships completely differently with ourselves and the "other." For it is this paradigm shift around love and union that will elevate humanity to experience the dimension of the gods.

We have long been steeped in an outdated social model of relating. Our relationship ideals and criticisms are based on the previous cycle, and these old ways will not support and serve the future of intimacy and union.

The biggest realization I have had, which has changed my relationships permanently, and allowed me to have a loving union which I highly value, is to know that the purpose of a relationship is for self-realization and spiritual evolution. It is not about feeling nice and supported all the time - but rather having someone else who will help you grow and heal and know the most powerful version of self possible with you.

When individuals or couples are struggling and come to me for work, we focus on each individual's connection and understanding of their life-force energy - or Kundalini. Education and experience are crucial for evolved relationships that will be propelled forward quickest through the willingness of both people to do the inner work. If one of the partners is too stubborn to take self-responsibility, then the relationship may be on a time-clock to timing-out. Though one person can do a lot of inner work, that inner work will either have to be mirrored by the partner, or that partner will find themselves somehow repelled out of the relationship. A strong bond or commitment where only one person is healing and advancing can only result in either an explosive severing or the rapid up-leveling of the one who was stubbornly resisting - as the other partner's energy pulls them forward(which is occasionally possible).

After focusing on one's life-force currents and how to feel and manage them, the work shifts to the energies between the two individuals in the union or magnetizing that "other" through various practices.

Tantric breath-work and kundalini exercises and visualizations get at the heart of any disconnects in a relationship and allow the couple to reconnect at the vital level of beingness - the life-force energy. By silently communicating energetically and through the practices Tantra teaches, couples can find their relationship propelled forward, healed from years of misunderstandings and emotional blocks, and sensually greatly enhanced - in a matter of a session or two. It is truly a beautiful thing.

After finding the connection again, the next step for a dedicated person or couple is to become more conscious during sexual union. This is the next most important area of focus and practice. Tantric Intimacy Alchemy and what I like to call Conscious Sexuality is where you become aware of the spiritual mechanics of orgasm in the body, learn to tap into them, and consciously move sexual energy to heal, bond more deeply, and potentize the orgasmic experience so that it goes beyond any previous experience of sex or climax either have experienced in the past.

The goal is to return to Divine Communion - the God-selves with one another. That is the end game - because when we, as a species, are functioning from high-level god-self unions, our entire reality changes. We solve problems differently. We are more compassionate humans and leaders. We access inspiration and creativity at a new level. We love, and we care. We walk this Earth like the King/Queen essence that we are - at the core of our beings - from an awake and integrated pineal and heart center. This is the greatest aspiration of my heart - to know humans, together, here, in this way.

As I lay naked in my bed each night, because I love the feel of my body on the sheets - whether my beloved is there or not - I am thrilled to know that even the breeze running through my open door onto my fingertips and toes is enough now, to send waves of ecstasy through me - without so much as a touch to any genital. My breakfast tea is a sweet tantalizer of energies as I wake from a dreamy night and enjoy the process of dressing, moving, and breathing in the body I so deeply care for and tend to. I recognize that every input can put me into a state of bliss and that I am the caretaker of what inputs I receive. Yes, I know I can transmute and transform, but I have also learned that it is simpler to manage one's space than to be constantly cleaning up after a leaky field.

It is good to remember that boundaries are both precious and necessary and non-existent in the multi-planes we are traversing together. It is important to dance in the paradox and not get lost. For that crazy knowing, I'm so grateful for my coaches - there to help reflect my reality so I can, again and again, self-correct and evolve as we go. I always wish to support my clients in the great empowerment project, both the Inner Alchemy of Transformation and the Alchemy of Sacred Relationship.

If you find yourself struggling in self-love or acceptance within a relationship or other relationship problems as could be labeled "toxic" by any of your friends or family - and you are stuck in the old paradigm of how a relationship "should be" (based on movies and television romance) - perhaps you'd like to take an evolutionary leap into an evolved relationship reality. Maybe it's time you stepped into the perspective where you are truly aware - with honor - that you are witnessing your partner's awakening journey - and they are witnessing yours. What a Bliss trip that is!

If you are alone and can't seem to attract "the one" - what if you knew how to find inner union - by managing your life-force energy, and that by doing so, you would likewise attract a match externally? Would you be all over that?

It's time for a Relationship Evolution into a world where the alchemy we experience is Sacred. It's been a hell of a journey to get here, and it is my deep honor to share with you decades of wisdom to enhance your relationship journey now. You already know it, and it is already happening. It is just time to tune into it.

STASIA BLISS

ABOUT THE AUTHOR

Stasia Bliss is a Life-Force Energy Educator and Sacred Relationship & Intimacy Coach specializing in Universal Kundalini Tantra and Inner Alchemy. She is an oracle, healer, mother, and mystic assisting in shifting human consciousness at this time to return to love through intimacy and vulnerable, authentic living and by choosing to evolve beyond previous frameworks and limiting mindsets consciously. Bringing together over two decades of relationship and life-force research, embodiment, and wisdom practices to assist in bringing forth the new relationship paradigm on Earth during this new ascension cycle. Stasia has authored more than 14 books, thousands of online articles, podcasts, and videos on consciousness, empowerment, and relationships; she works one-on-one with couples and individuals and is the owner and educator of BlissMe, an online Awakening Resource App to support her work.

Links: blissinthehouse.com and the family mandala. space

16

IN THIS WORLD, NOT OF IT

BY: LEZLIE MITCHELL

Connecting Dreams and Waking Life

W hen I was seven years old, I had the unique opportunity to spend the night in a museum. I was told that one child out of each school in the district was chosen for the special opportunity to spend the night next to an ancient mummy and learn all about Egypt. You see, his exhibit was in town, and since I was in my school's gifted and talented program, my teacher decided to submit me. At the time, I didn't realize how unusual this experience was. How could I? Years later, though, I was able to see how it played a part in furthering the course I was already set upon, that of the Mystic. After my night in the museum, something strange happened. I woke up one morning with one of my eyes sealed shut. No matter what I did, I couldn't open it. I was hospitalized overnight for it and placed on an IV. That night, I remember having a dream that has stuck with me until this day. I saw a hand above me coming from the light in the dream. It was inviting me to come into the light.

As I grabbed the hand and began to ascend, another hand pulled my feet from the darkness beneath me. I was pulled and tugged between the two in the dream until finally, I woke up.

Even at seven, I knew this dream had great significance for my life. My only lens at the time was that of Evangelical Christianity, and so I viewed it as God and the Devil fighting over my soul. Though that interpretation still rings true for me in many ways today, it has broadened some. As my path took me beyond the church doors and into other spiritual houses and philosophies, my obsession with seeking was activated. Christ said, *"Ask, and it will be given to you; seek, and you will find; knock, and the door will be opened to you."* The common questions like: who am I?, why am I here? And what is this place? It began to haunt me in the best way possible. The commonly accepted explanations all spoon-fed to us didn't satisfy me, and I knew there was more in the deepest parts of me. Like most of us, I was told that we would never know things. However, I had a teacher hear me, and she shared a nugget with me from Einstein. He said, *"It's not that I'm so smart; I just stick with a problem longer."* So, I decided early in life that this seeming mystery called life was something I would stick with and seek to understand until my last breath.

However, I chose to hide in the shadows for most of my life instead of standing firmly in the light. I learned to do this due to painful experiences in the past where standing in the light and operating in my gifts meant becoming an outcast, and if there was one thing I wanted in my youth, it was to be loved and accepted. I didn't want to risk getting uninvited, like the time in 7th grade when I shared a detailed dream with a friend I had of her that had actually happened a week prior, unknown to me. When she went home to tell her mom, she said I was no longer welcome in their home because a gift like that was not from God but from the devil. So I hid. But I've come to realize that hiding makes me sick. If I can't operate as the being I was created to be and share the gifts that were imprinted within my DNA, then it eats at me.

Years of hiding contributed to depression, anxiety, and eating disorders. It led to chasing the world's illusions like fame for fame's sake. I realized I couldn't live that way, it seemed such a sad way to exist, and it felt it go against my divine purpose. And now, after years of hiding and trying to fit into the box that was molded around me by various programmers, I know I am here to help deprogram and free others from the box.

Like my dream in the hospital as a child, we are pushed and pulled within a duality matrix called Earth. Haven't you noticed? I know I have. I have been pulled in every direction: up and down, left and right, big and small. The full spectrum of human duality pushes us to be more masculine or feminine, lean towards good, and resist evil, and the list of polarity goes on indefinitely.

And then there is your dream life and your waking life, which is where my life experiences placed my attention - on my dreams, and how waking up and remembering my dreams was like waking up in reality and remembering the life I came here to live.

Roughly ten years ago, I had another dream that has stuck with me. I remember waking up off the ground and standing up slowly as I looked around my environment in this dream. On the ground was a sea of people sleeping, thousands of them as far as I could see in every direction. As I continued to look around me, I saw maybe a dozen other people in my immediate area rise up from their slumber too. Then I woke up on this side of the veil.

This dream was the conscious trigger of my awakening process. It was an easy dream to interpret, that I was awake and most of the people around me were sleeping. It also revealed that I wasn't alone though I was greatly outnumbered. Others were waking up. Since that dream, it has been a gradual awakening process for me in my waking life.

I have experienced the process of awakening in my life is sometimes slow and subtle, and at other times - at other stages of awareness - a more brutal push. It's so similar to your sick child or newborn baby beginning to wake up from a long nap. You've been by their side, watching them sleep with loving-kindness. As they begin to yawn and stretch, you wouldn't shake them to wake them up faster if you cared about them, would you? No. You would let them wake up one stretch at a time, continuing to watch with attention. Now, if there were some emergency and your sick child or newborn baby clearly needed you, then you would probably step in to help. For me, some stages have been slow and steady awareness coming, and other times life has smacked me across the face. I have to remember that everyone wakes up in their own time, in different ways.

The oldest souls and the greatest Masters all start this journey called life as a baby. At some point, I imagine we all begin to notice that life may not be what it seems. For me, I began to notice things that others write off as coincidence or randomness. Synchronicities became the new "norm." My intuition started buzzing more and more that something was amiss with the world. I painstakingly began to ask questions, as I assume all seekers do, some hard questions and some seemingly simpler ones. And somehow, the answers have largely revealed themselves, the information comes. The process, to me, feels like the game we played as children, Hide-and-Seek. But now we are playing the game for much higher stakes.

One of my favorite dream quotes is something like: a dream uninterpreted is like a letter unopened. The gift of dream interpretation has helped me face my shadow self, given me helpful warnings, and brought to the surface things that I try to ignore in my waking life. My dreams had allowed me a front-row seat to see planets re-align, meet my daughter before she was born, and see my life purpose revealed with great clarity. The benefits of this gift continue to unfold in my life, and I am grateful that I can assist other Artists and Starseeds with connecting the dots between their dreams and waking life.

<u>Saying:</u>

"We agreed to experience everything incarnating on Earth, including the deep wounding. But we also came here to heal those wounds so that we can create a new template within ourselves and the collective."

—Radhaa

LEZLIE MITCHELL (B.MSC, B.A. ENGLISH)

ABOUT THE AUTHOR

Lezlie Mitchell is a prolific storyteller through multiple creative streams, including writing, acting, and modeling. She has appeared in numerous print ads and national commercials for popular brands like Ancestry, AT&T, MTV, Albertsons, Orbit Gum, Livestrong, and Fossil. Lezlie has been featured in the NY Post, NPR, and Voyage LA for her range of work.

Known for her wisdom, creativity, and highly intuitive nature, Lezlie has walked the Mystic path since early childhood. She was raised in a devout Christian home and began studying the work of Christ and the Essenes early on. She is of the Rose

Lineage and a professionally trained Metaphysician. She finds great joy in helping others connect the dots between their dreams and waking life through various healing modalities, including dreamwork, prayer, and energy transmutation.

Connect with her at www.LoveLezlie.com

17

TRANQUIL COMPANION

BY: MAUREEN KELLE

How I Came To Tranquil Companion

I had not intended to go down the healing path. It all began with a Rottweiler I had named Amalia. She was an athlete doing agility, tracking, obedience, hospice. She was a registered therapy dog with Therapy Dogs International. Everything I could do with her we did together. Occasionally, she would get injured, and I did not want to give her drugs. I started looking for alternative remedies. I had researched several alternative remedies and started down the path of holistic remedies for Amalia.

Later on down the road, I had gotten another Rottweiler, and her name was Grace. I had special bonds with both of these dogs. But Grace had something that she needed to communicate with me. I felt this. One day, I went to an animal communicator doing Communications for people and their animals inside a dog and cat Boutique. I took Amalia and Grace there, and through the communicator, Grace told me that I was given a "special gift" and that I should learn energy healing and take Reiki. I did not know what Reiki was, so I did some research. I located a Reiki master and took the level one attunement. During the introductions at the beginning of the course, I expressed an interest in converting what I learned to heal animals. A woman in the group told me about a certification program that dealt with healing animals on an energetic level. After my level one Reiki Attunement, I looked for this certificate program that the lady at the Reiki class had told me about. I proceeded to get certified in all four levels and became a Healing Touch for Animals™ practitioner. I continue to get education in as many non-invasive modalities as possible.

Today I work on humans and animals both remotely and in person. I take all of the modalities that I've learned and combine them into a unique blend of Integrative therapies I call the "Tranquil Companion Technique." I blend my energetic modalities for humans, picking and choosing intuitively what the client needs at the session. I use non-invasive tools such as Sound, Photonic Health, Biomat, Magnetic therapy, Crystal therapy, Essential oils, Light Pad therapy, Acupressure, Equine iridology, and Dowsing, to name a few.

How I Connect with my Animal Clients

I have three horses and one dog at the time of this writing. All my horses came to me with emotional baggage. You can read Princess Lacey's story on my Tranquil Companion Facebook page, dated June 12th, 2018. At the time of this writing, Miss Sophie is 34 a year old Quarter horse. Although she wasn't abused, she had nutritional issues and neglected physical needs before arriving at the rescue. The rescue that I got Sophie and Lacy from was unable to keep up with Sophie's nutritional needs, and she was taken out of the lessons program and just put out to pasture. By the time I had gotten her, she was too thin to ride and was losing weight.

I adopted Sophie and Lacey within months of each other. They were best friends, and they have not been separated since I adopted them ten years ago. When I got Sophie, I put her on a nutritional program, and she put on some healthy weight. In a few months, she could carry a rider, and I took lessons to learn how to ride her from that day until she was 32. I rode her on countless trails. Now I walk Sophie and Lacey by hand on the trails at the boarding facility that I keep them at. I also have a Paso Fino horse named Elegancia, as "Pea." I have entrusted my life to this horse.

Elegancia is my everyday mount. She is 15 years old at the time of this writing. She was labeled a dangerous angry mare that doesn't like anyone or anything, but she likes me! I've had this little girl for six years, and only has she started to trust me in the past two years. She has been so misunderstood and strong-armed, forced to do things that you didn't want to do. I've given her choices, Freedom, love, patience, and understanding. She's giving me Trust. Now I have Carmen Francesca, the only Rottweiler I have left. Miss Carmen has no issues and is the ultimate love bunny. She's my companion that I take almost everywhere I go. She walks with the horses when I take them on the trails at the boarding stable that they are at.

These four animals have taught me how to communicate with them on different emotional levels to satisfy their emotional and physical needs. I have taken these lessons with me to use on my animal clients. Each of them displays some attributes that I can connect emotionally with my animal clients and better understand them to assist in their healing process.

Domestic animals' purpose in most cases is to be our

companions. It is not an easy task. As our companions, these animals comfort us, absorb our anxiety, pain, suffering, and trauma. They only asked for love in return. But, what about these dense, heavy emotions and energies that we inadvertently inflict on our animals? Energetically these emotions can cause emotional and physical imbalances in our animals that can manifest into serious issues if not released. Think about it. Humans have all sorts of releases for tension and anxiety, grief and pain. We can go to the gym, run, bike ride, Etc. to escape or relieve the pressure. Animals don't have that option. So they may exhibit behavioral issues, self-mutilation, inappropriate deification, and even physical issues such as hot spots. Here at Tranquil Companion, I address these issues and allow the animal to release these toxic dense energies so that they can continue to be the companion they were purposed to be. I believe each animal has a journey sometimes. They reach an obstacle in their path. I'm here to remove those obstacles so they can continue their journey and their Soul's purpose.

Working With Humans

Most of my credentials are designed to work for humans, and I had to redesign the applications to work with animals. My animal clients' persons have asked me if I work on people. To which I would answer," no, definitely not." It wasn't until about two years ago a client asked me why not? I stated that most humans don't understand energy work, expect an instant miracle, and don't do what I suggest. To which the client said to me, "if they are asking you for help, they are prepared for a remedy, why would you turn them away?." It hit me in the head like a two-by-four, and I thought to myself, who am I to judge the ones that come to me for help. A valuable lesson that I learned. I am a

Healer, and this is the gift I was given. So in the past couple of years, I have started working on humans that seek me out for comfort from emotional and physical pain. I have experienced great joy in the practical healing of humans. All that have come to me have experienced some relief, whether emotional, physical, or both. My passion, goal, and Soul's purpose is to facilitate self-healing to those in need who come for help.

Case Study

When I first started my business at Tranquil Companion in 2012/2013, I encountered mostly animals with emotional baggage. A particular case comes to mind and probably the most intense case in all the years that I've been working in my business to date.

There was a woman I would call her D and her gelding horse that I will call Buddy. Buddy had suffered an emotional wound a year or so before she had contacted me. Buddy's brother had gotten stolen from the stall next to his during the night. Buddy's brother was the herd leader. All of a sudden, not only did Buddy have the grief of losing his brother and best friend, but the rest of the herd was looking to Buddy for leadership, which buddy was not prepared to handle. As a result, he became depressed and angry and seemed detached from D. No matter how much she tried to engage him. He wouldn't respond. He was shut down.

I came to the stable one afternoon to work on him. I used the technique that I had learned in one of the disciplines in which there is a letting go of emotional baggage. I always involve the animals' person to feel the emotions being released when performing this. It creates compassion for the animals' situation, but it creates a bond for them as they have helped relieve their emotional pain. We were in the last stall of the barn. All the other stalls were filled with people grooming their horses for riding or lessons. As Buddy let go of the emotional baggage one by one, we, myself and D, felt intense anger, then intense grief, and finally extreme sadness. After Buddy had released all of these emotions, we let him chill for a moment. As I looked around at the other people, I noticed everyone, including myself and D, had been crying. I feel that Everyone in the barn felt Buddy's extreme sadness as he let it go. I'm happy to report that after that release, he turned out to be the happy, confident, and carefree horse that he was before the emotional wound had occurred. It was one of my happiest experiences.

Another case comes to mind. Tranquil Companion offers a service to existing clients that enables an animal to transition during euthanasia. It allows the animal to make the transition peaceful and stress-free. A dog client who was getting ready to transition had not barked or run around and played since his pack-mate had transitioned a year or two earlier. At the veterinary office where this dog was making his transition as the transition process was occurring, I saw in my mind's eye this dog running across the bridge barking and wagging his tail, greeting another dog that was waiting on the other side. I had described this dog to the owners, and as it turns out, this other dog that was across the bridge was, in fact, the pack-mate that had transitioned the previous year or two before. As this dog transitioned, He barked, and his tail was wagging, and his feet were moving as if he was running as he took his last breath. I was so deeply honored and truly touched that I could facilitate this transition peacefully and happily because this is the last Act of love that humans can do for their best companion.

MAUREEN KELLER

ABOUT THE AUTHOR

Maureen Keller is the owner of Tranquil Companion products and services. She is an Integrative therapy practitioner, an Equine Iridologist, and an Equine bodywork massage therapist, working on animals and people. Using Energy Medicine and non-invasive tools such as essential oils, magnetic, tuning fork, far infrared acupressure, crystal therapies, and more to integrate balance clear energy blocks to relieve pain, stress, and anxiety. It helps the animal recover from injury and illness and emotional trauma and abuse issues to reduce stress and anxiety, clarify appropriate behavior, relieve pain, and achieve a quality of life with chronic illness or disease. For humans, energy therapies such as Pranic healing, Reiki, crystals, and photonic health relieve emotional and physical pain, stress, and anxiety. She works remotely and personally, fully trained and certified in all four Healing Touch for Animals. Advanced Reiki Techniques, Honors Graduate from Ellen Collison school of Equine Iridology, Pranic Healing, Level One, Certification in Young Living Oil application for animals, Advanced Pranic Healing. Maureen is in the process of acquiring certification to be a Masterson Method Equine Bodywork and Massage. See Tranquil Companion Facebook page. Keep unconditional love in your heart and an open mind.

Text or call **618-972-8267** for prices on products and services or book an appointment.

18

SPINNING GODDESS HEALER

BY: DANIELLE SCHRECK

T he human body's Intelligence is beyond extraordinary as to what it's capable of. Many people, like myself, come to a place in their life where they begin this slow initiation process of learning how powerful they truly are.

Dissatisfaction in Corporate America

In my case, I arrived at an internal dissatisfaction in my mid-twenties where I began to question everything, and I knew an awakening started to occur. I feel that there was so much more out there for me despite being quite alone during that time. Working in corporate America served as a catalyst to push through challenges in expanding my mind in my desire to leave this Matrix of the 9-5.

People along that path introduced me to personal development and spiritual matters. As I was exploring and learning about entrepreneurship while listening to people like Abraham Hicks and reading books like "The Power of Now," it all inspired me and sent me down a rabbit hole. I learned so much in those years. As I was dabbling and slowly growing through the different stages and phases, I realized everything was always bridging together. Yet, it felt at many times, there was another level to unfold before I could move forward.

Some days were easier than others, but I just kept going as I embraced the satisfaction of each synchronistic experience, guiding me forward as though a higher power had taken over.

Understanding My Natural Inquisitiveness

This ultimately led me to learn about different Holistic modalities that intrigued me deeply. I loved to share my findings with individuals that would be open to hearing my findings or bits of information I read. I had met many people over the years through many jobs that always seemed to be in my life at the right place and time. This synchronistic experience really bridged my awareness of knowing when I was on an "on" or "off" path and thus helped hone in my awareness of what's meant for me or not. It really helped me understand that my natural inquisitiveness was meant to help and inspire others as a catalyst.

Seeking Healing and Inner Work

For whatever reason, you seek Healing, whether it's by design in your approach or because the Western world has pushed you to find solutions outside the box in what some would call "Unorthodox," and just know your path will always be unique to you.

I teach others to be patient with themselves, just as I have to be patient with myself as I learn and journey through the process. As I began to listen to the whispers of the soul, I realized how intuitively guided I am, and that includes the people who step in and out of my life as conduits or messengers. Learning to trust my intuition and connecting to a higher power feels magical and fun. Whenever I got off course, I could really feel it, and it would also impact my ways of thinking and vibrational energy. It would throw me into a loop, and in some ways, I can say it taught me the importance of managing my vibration mentally, emotionally, physically, and spiritually. It's something that I work on daily and be mindful of once I own my co-creator abilities. A decade later, I had a broad interest in Holistic Healing and dynamic perception. However, I await with no clear direction on where to start or my path.

Meeting my Mentors and Healers

Things rapidly changed when I started my healing work with Radhaa Nilia of Goddess Code Academy and Maya the Shaman (Lemurian healer). I practiced my inner work. Radhaa had recommended trying Pendulum Healing with another Healer and the combination of all these sessions really quickly accelerated my Healing. It was then I realized how easily my body was receiving the clearings. It resonated so much with me, and I became inquisitive to learn using the Pendulum myself.

My Pendulum Healing at Goddess Code Academy

I enrolled through the Goddess Code Academy, where I learned about the "Spinning Goddess" with Radhaa, my teacher, and Goddess Activations™ original Creatrix. I began learning this special Divination Tool in my after hours of work. I had spent 2021 learning how to clear, use my intention, and trust in the Creator to intuitively guide me. The process was very natural for me, and through the training, I had volunteered to Spin with a Group Radhaa created called "Spinning to Heal the World." We'd meet once or a few times a month on behalf to "Spin to Heal the World" and to clear dark energies impacting Humanity. The results have been powerful! When a group of two or more come together, it helps to clear the energies to swing in favor of our highest timeline for the Collective. We would also spin on topics related to our personal lives, and the positive results kept coming in! It inspired me to keep going, and I'd eagerly practiced alone or with others. During this time, I also became a Contributing Writer in the "Pillars of Light: Stories of Goddess Activations."

I had been practicing and helping some contributing writers through video interviews through Radhaa Publishing House, and the results continued to amaze me. One of the women I had never met received results from a clearing I've done, and it was my intuitive verbiage that was spot on. The day after, I received the great news of how the session helped her, which surprised and pleased me! Her testimony felt like a complete miracle, thus instilling a stronger belief in how powerful Pendulum Healing truly is.

I Become a Certified "Spinning Goddess" Practitioner Healer

Upon Graduating from the Goddess Code Academy, I was guided to begin helping those I personally know by offering my services officially to clients privately and through my Etsy Shop. I began to truly understand the power of intentions and how important personal vibrational frequency is. To set no expectations, yet showing up as a vessel for the Creator to pour into and receive the discernment to understand as it would unfold moment by moment. I've learned to surrender and allow the unfolding through its natural course.

"Spinning Goddess Healer" Feedback

The feedback and blessings of "Spinning Goddess by Goddess Code Academy" have brought into my life unique, inspiring, and deeply healing energies for me.

"It is when we heal ourselves we help heal the world!"

My clients and I altogether benefit from Spinning Goddess. For example, financial support flowed in when I decided to get out of corporate America and step into the spinning course to transition work and become sovereign. Today, I quit my full-time job in corporate America and am officially a full-time Spinning Goddess Practitioner on 1-1 sessions with clients, and you can find me on Etsy. I am overjoyed by these Cosmic blessings. Thank you, Goddess Venus! Goddess Venus is my personal Goddess; I shared in my story at "Pillars of Light: Stories of Goddess Activations."

Radhaa is an incredible mentor, and I highly encourage you to explore and seek ways to try any course offered by Radhaa at Goddess Code Academy. There are many possibilities of healing work offered. Try it, and it may just work magic for you! (Just as it did for me!) Allow your inner discernment to choose what type of healing work resonates with you. The real Healing is doing the inner work and enjoying yourself during the process. May this collaborative book of Healers give you a unique perspective to do just that. Wishing you the highest timeline of peace and love as you transform into the best version of yourself!

Sayings:

"I believe in the miracles of Energy Healing. It has shown me and many others that what we shift from within — shifts in our outer reality."

— Radhaa Nilia

DANIELLE SCHRECK

ABOUT THE AUTHOR

Danielle Schreck is a Certified Spinning Goddess Practitioner healer graduate of Goddess Code Academy. She offers her 1-1 sessions to anyone who wishes to clear blockages of any kind.

Danielle is a co-author of "Energy Healing and Soul Medicine," book. She is a contributing Writer to books "Pillars of Light: Stories of Goddess Activations," and the forthcoming book "Infinite Cosmic Records: Sacred Doorways to Healing & Remembering,"(Summer 2022).

You can find Danielle by visiting her Etsy store at: https://www.etsy.com/shop/AphroditeHeartVibes?ref=profile_header

19

GODDESS ACTIVATIONS™
BY: RADHAA NILIA

The Lost Goddess

I believe in the power of the Divine Feminine. In ancient times, there were Priestess Temples globally. These sacred feminine Temples have been destroyed, their teachings and the initiations lost in the rubble. Rituals of profound connection are forgotten, leaving fractures in the hearts and minds of women, men, and society. This crack in our collective psyche seemed to become bigger and bigger as the patriarchy grew and grew. I feel that returning to the temple and bringing back the Codes of the Goddess is the missing link.

The divine feminine Essence is needed now more than ever in our world. It is part of my Dharma to bring back Goddess energy, anchor it into this Planet, and share it with all women ready to receive it through my original healing modality called Goddess Activations™. Through this work, we balance the scales and bring back the true Rose Code Essence of the divine feminine through Goddess Activations™.

Goddess Found

The Goddess has been with me my whole life, even before birth. My parents named me after RadhaKrsna, Goddess of Love and Devotion. As romantic as that sounds, the deeper meaning is devotion to the Divine, devotion to my life's calling and mission. I've had a lifelong cosmic love affair with the Goddess in her many forms. SHE has been there for me when I call upon HER. As a child, my mom took me to the Goddess temples and introduced me to the Goddesses.

Warrior Goddess

In my early childhood, my mom left America and brought me to the very top of the Cordillera Mountains in Maharlika (the Philippines) to live with the natives when I was just three and a half years old. In these mountains, I met Goddess Gaia herself. I learned of the Goddess of nature named Maria Makiling, a Filipina Goddess who was the guardian of the Maria Makiling Mountains in Laguna. Yet, she is the nature Goddess of Lemuria, a revered Goddess of the Philippines for those who can remember.

In these mountains, I felt the Spirit of the Goddess all around me. The natives of these lands are aligned with the elementals, calling "Papa Sky, Momma Earth/Goddess Earth." Unspoiled lands, no distortion or corruption had touched this land at that time. To me, this place was Heaven on Earth. The indigenous people welcomed my mother, baby brother, and myself. We came alone to see them. They gifted and adored my mother with their spiritual handmade jewelry and clothing. I recall the gifts: a necklace made of the bones of a snake, beaded bracelets, and handwoven fabric wrapped around as sarongs.

They took my mother into their sacred cave of the dead, where they honor their indigenous ancestors. They invited my mom to meditate in this sacred space, honor the ancestors, and learn to transcend fear into personal power. My mother took their invitation and meditated for days in the cafe while my brother and I were cared for most lovingly. We spent our days in the hot spring waters of the jungle and ate with our hands off of large bamboo leaves. We lived with the rhythm of nature and experienced what we call bliss.

The Igorots, Indigenous People of Maharlika

The Igorots were known as the Warrior people. They are ancestral land keepers who have known their ancient sacred lands for many generations and can never be dominated. They never gave themselves easily to the Spanish conquerors who invaded. Instead, they fought with fierce courage and bravely.

The Igorot people were unwilling to give their Sovereign Rights over through the rampant colonization. Why should they bow to intruders when they were the keepers of the land. They were connected to the Spirit of Mother Gaia and assigned to live on these lands. Their profound connection with Mother Gaia made them courageous Warriors, and they would not let abusers conquer them or HER.

They were undefeated. Despite not having guns or matching weapons, their Spirit and dedication to keeping their rights to live their indigenous ways were free. At the same time, the lowlanders were easily taken over and colonized beyond recognition. Traditional ways were long forgotten as they were beaten with bibles and shame-ridden for being savages.

For the Igorots, the mountain women were Matriarchs who instructed the men to cut the heads of their enemies, shrink them and wear them on their belts. And they became known as headhunters to the conquistadors, who, although they had guns and greater weapons than the Igorots, did not dare to face the fierceness of the Igorot's Spirit.

Being amongst the Igorots was a lesson in staying true to one's Spirit. They imprinted the Warrior Spirit in me that would later serve me well. These indigenous warriors reminded me of the fierce Goddess Kali. Yet, these tribes of people were the most kind and loving ones. They were gentle souls to those with good intentions and good hearts and were hospitable and opened their arms and received us as their own. The Igorots felt like family to me. Pure hearts, clean minds. No projections, just Love. I was truly blessed to have experienced the purest meaning of Universal Love and the abundance of nature in the East. So grateful for this pure, innocent experience, I knew this is something that no matter what I went through in my life, I could always come back to this knowledge as it was imprinted within my very being. The Igorots gave me a boon, a blessing as a child, that no matter what kind of challenges I would endure, I would always have the Spirit of the Sovereign Warrior.

Sovereign Warrior roots come back again and again throughout my life. This sacred imprint would serve me well in facing the darkness. I would always have a portal of innocence I could come back to. This initiation on top of the great Cordillera Mountains with the untouched people of the lands anchored me deeply into Mother Gaia Codes, keeping my connection to HER, the cord connected deep into the Earth and into the Crystal Core; at the very center would be my roots to this world.

Resurrecting my Inner Goddess

Coming back to America was so tumultuous. Parents

divorced. Eleven schools before middle school. I felt uprooted regularly and picked apart by all my new teachers and the kids because starting over and over at a new school is never easy. Always the weirdo, the little Starseed who just could not, would not fit in. So by the time I got to high school, I stopped trying to fit in with kids my age. I started going to college taking elective classes that I wanted. Filmmaking and memoir writing classes. I could not believe how much more I felt at home with elders than with the kids at my school.

In my elective classes, they were filled with wise women with white hair. I was particularly drawn to the Crones. I found Crone medicine to be so healing. I felt so much comfort and Love in their presence, and I learned so much from them. I loved hearing their stories so much in the class. I, too, wished to live a full and glorious life of adventure. I also understood that they had endured much. They often spoke of Love, as many of them were now widows. I could listen to them forever, and I knew I had to get them on film. I ended up doing a documentary called "Women in Love." I saw the sacred Crone Goddess in each woman. I adored them. Later, when we had a screening at the theater, the film became very controversial. Women who attended cried with the understanding of the pain and betrayal that some of these women had to go through, while some men stomped out of the theater, unable to be with the raw, real truth of the feminine journey.

When I made the film, I had not much experience with relationships, neither good nor bad. I was curious and asked questions about their lives, loves, and what they had learned. I wanted so much to learn, to understand what relationships meant and what they meant to these beautiful Crones who had undergone many initiations over their lifetime. I had always known that the path of the Goddess was indeed one of great initiations and activations. In the depths of my youth, I craved a deeper and more meaningful feminine connection. I had already encountered so much distorted, wounded, and even deeply scarring abuse from the punishing feminine. I was aware of how distorted the divine feminine energy had become. The abuse I received from a feminine caregiver who did not love herself and, in turn, told me that no one loved me as a child was a wound that I was on a mission to heal from. The wound went so very deep and felt reflected in my romantic relationships that would come. I went through life feeling this horrible feeling of being unloved and unloveable. It did not matter if people said they loved me. I could not receive it. I was so blocked and burdened with this terrible feeling.

I desired to break the cures placed on me, and I also desired to bring women together, healing so that this feminine self-hatred would end. I craved the temple of the Goddess in my heart and soul. I went to red tents, women's workshops, Goddess seminars, and Feminine Leadership workshops. I wanted to be amongst women. I wanted to share Love and friendship that was deeper and more meaningful.

I also wanted to tend to my very deep wounding, which led to being certified in over a dozen holistic healing modalities as a practitioner and teacher. As much as I struggled with these internal wounds, I thank them for leading me to my higher purpose. As Rumi says, the wound is where the light enters. The Goddess knows that only through thorns does the rose, Bloom. And the long and windy path of exploring my thorns through the healing journey led me to create "Goddess Code Academy," A Mystical School for the Divine Feminine, the home of Goddess Activations™.

I thank the great Igorot women, who, to me, were manifestations of Goddesses. Feminine Igorots were matriarchs but had the qualities of the Goddesses, as their souls filled with light that both soothed and inspired me never to give up. This early childhood experience, from the meaning of my name and childhood upbringing, became initiations to my life that led me to the creation of an original modality called Goddess Activations™."

What is Goddess Activations™?

Goddess Activations is a living light energy transmission filled with pure Goddess Code™ frequencies. It is a sacred journey into the Goddess's heart of the feminine where we tap into the soul essence of the feminine blueprint. It is different from any other healing modality I've ever experienced. Being a Certified Advanced Teacher and Practitioner in multiple healing modalities, I feel grateful to learn. Yet, I felt something was missing that resonated with my soul until I was awakened to Goddess Activations™.

I enjoy teaching women the power of Goddess Archetypes and embodying them through the guidance I offered with an easy template to follow. It worked for my clients and me. The Goddess Activations™ awakens the Goddess Codes™, which currently lie dormant inside you. It's true. We have been tampered with on many levels, including our original DNA. So much time has passed, but now we must come to reclaim what truly belongs to us. It is time to Remember your divinity, innate gifts, inner truth, and personal power with the boon of the Goddesses.

I love to see women, Bloom, just as a Rose blooms through its thorns. It is for women ready to rise from within their own Goddess Heart. In witnessing every thorn, heartache, rejection and hurt, and betrayal and offering it at the altar, transmuting it into the most beautiful light. There is no judgment as to what comes up in a session because just about anything and every-thing does. It's multidimensional healing, working on past, present, future, and parallel lifetimes.

Pillars of Light: Goddess Activations™

I got the download that it was essential to bring back the original blueprint of the "Pillars of Light" through the Goddess Activations™. I teach Goddess Archetypes to nurture and empower the feminine through this powerful Essence of the Goddess using my method, Goddess Activations™. It is vital in awakening all aspects of the feminine. The balance of our world depends on it. It is essential to learn about the various Goddesses, who they are, their offerings, gifts, and boons. One can learn how to heal oneself and others through this feminine modality. My mission is to further bring this work to millions of women worldwide through Goddess Code Academy™. A working temple offering devotion serves as a divine remem-brance of where we once were and where we want to be. The temple is a service to Mother Gaia to help raise the frequency on this Earth. It's a reminder that we are not alone and have our sisters, soul families, and communities. As each one of us heals and raises our vibration, we offer this gift of Love, healing, and remembering to the collective.

What is a Goddess Code™?

The "Goddess Code' is a Key that unlocks the ability to awaken the dormant Codes within. The Goddess Code™ has unique activations that allow people to create physical manifes-tations even faster. In true Essence, Goddess Activations™ unlocks the Goddess Codes™. It is essential to bring back the original integrity of our Pillars of Light through Goddess Activations™. I use many Goddess Healing and Clearing tools. One of my favorites is "Spinning Goddess™, a feminine form of Pendulum Healing."

What is Spinning Goddess™?

We teach Spinning Goddess™ at Goddess Code Academy. It's a fun and easy way to clear and reprogram old beliefs, traumas, vows, oaths, and unwanted commitments while working with Goddess Energy. You can get trained and certified at Goddess Code Academy as a Spinning Goddess practitioner and Activator.

Journey to Your Inner Goddess

My clients tell me that Goddess Activations™ sessions are unlike anything they've ever experienced before. In a session, I work with a series of Ancient Goddess Archetypes on a multidimensional level, resulting in a clearing healing on the heart wounds and soul level. Everything you need is already inside you, lying dormant. As your Goddess Guide, I help activate the Goddess Code™ within and awaken the Goddess Archetype needed in that session.

Re-Coding with Goddess Activations™

This work deeply reprograms and re-patterns back to the original Soul Blueprint. Clearing away all the distortions and sabotage patterns and beliefs keeping you hostage in a timeline or reality you don't desire. When you step into the sacred initiations through Goddess Activations™, you may experience yourself in a brand new way. Awakened. Sessions are not cookie-cutter but highly intuitive. I tune in with the client's energy 48 hours before a session. When it's time for the session, I do all the intuitive downloads from the Creator's Heart. It's a very interactive session, where I can see past lives and describe them to clear current issues.

No two sessions are ever the same. We decide the Goddess who will be working with you beforehand. If you don't know, I will intuitively connect with the help of your higher self, and together, we choose as this has always been successful. During our session, I start with a thirty-minute deep clearing for you. Clearing the space so that we can connect with the Goddess deeper. Then we move into your Infinite Cosmic Records™ to meet the Goddess specifically working with you. As we connect with your Goddess, I will receive an influx of information that will be very specific and valuable as a conduit of the Goddess herself. The Goddess will provide you with her blessings in many areas specific to your needs. The healing extends to all other areas of life, often that people don't even expect. The true Essence of the Goddess will inspire, awaken, and elevate your everyday reality. You will restore your confidence as you work with your Goddess and align with her high frequency. It enables you to manifest your desires much easier in the physical world. Goddess Activations™ offers clearing, healing, and cosmic messages. I believe that everyone has their zone of genius, and Goddess Activations™ happens to be mine. I work as a midwife, a Soul ally, walking side by side through the process of unraveling the old stories, beliefs, and cellular memories so that the birth of the Priestess within may birth. Making way for a clearer channel from within.

Some things you can expect to experience in sessions are:

Karmic Clearing

Activate Creativity

Manifest Abundance

Restore your Original Blueprint

Remember your Soul's Purpose and Mission

Heal Your Heart Chakra

Heal your Inner Child

Ignite Courage

Heal your Womb

Call Back Your Light, Essence, & Power

Restore Soul Fragments & Self-honor

Help Release Unwanted Past Lives

Restore Inner Trust

Activate Confidence, Self-love & Beauty

Awaken your Psychic Gifts

Inspires you to Move Forward In Life

Cord Clearing with Ex-partners or Lovers

Release Negative Attachments & Entities

Claim your Self Empowerment

Attract Love and Happiness

Heal your Finances

Elevate your Life

I believe that everyone has their zone of genius, and Goddess Activations™ happens to be my way of serving. For more information about my Goddess Healing Modality, you can read my book, **Pillars of Light: Goddess Activations™**, where women who've experienced Goddess Activation™ share their experiences and stories with their Goddess Archetypes. It's a book filled with wisdom, inspiration, and beauty.

The Goddess Activations™ is an invitation to fall in Love with yourself again. Women who walk through these temple doors with open hearts and sincerity receive Soul medicine. When you learn this sacred healing modality, you become a Certified Goddess Activator™.

I've had many women tell me how this work has brought them back to feeling confident and in touch with themselves. That is what I want for everyone. However, that may come. In my heart, I know the future is brighter than we could ever imagine. And these are the times that we all need support. We are here to be that for one another. And it is true that when you search, you shall find. I hope you find the healer of your dreams in this book that can serve you.

In Goddess Love,

Radhaa

~

RADHAA NILIA

ABOUT THE AUTHOR

Radhaa Nilia is a Feminine Leader, Creatrix of "Goddess Code Academy: A Mystical school for the Divine Feminine." An online temple where she teaches her original modality, Goddess Activations™: https://radhaanilia.net/goddess-activations/

She is a multimedia Artist, Coach, Teacher, Curator, and Author of the Awakening Starseeds book series bringing together voices worldwide to share their stories. Her books can be found at Amazon, Barnes & Noble, Walmart, Target,

Additionally, *Radhaa* is the founder of Radhaa Publishing House and a contributing writer for various online magazines such as Huffington Post, Elephant Journal, Splash Magazine and continues to Curate collaborative books for Authors' voices to shine through.

To find Radhaa go to: www.RadhaaNilia.net

Sayings:

"People ask me what it takes to heal. Sincerity, the desire to heal, showing up, facing the shadows, looking at lineage wounds, and tracking karmic looping. Understanding there are layers and dimensions at play. Working with a qualified professional healer who has these understandings and is thorough, diligent and sincere creates positive results. Being patient with the process as the wound pains come to the surface, as it may get worse before it gets better. But this is what it takes to heal and it's all part of the healing journey. So never stop. Keep on healing your wounds and celebrate the freedom of its offering."

—Radhaa Nilia

ABOUT RADHAA PUBLISHING HOUSE

BECOME AN AUTHOR, or A CONTRIBUTING WRITER

Radhaa Publishing House is a holistic publishing company that focuses on helping heart-centered, mind-expanding, truth-telling authors get their work out into the world. Our focus is on collaborative book series and memoirs. We thrive on supporting our authors and contributing writers throughout this journey, empowering them to step into their divine and authentic voice while sharing their truth with the world. We especially celebrate cultural diversity worldwide, and we believe in weaving international voices to come together.

How are we different?

Many collaborative publishing companies bundle the authors together so that they don't receive individual credit and acknowledgment. We make sure each Author is seen and heard and can be found easily. This has led to authors telling us that they have received more traffic and business and clients on their websites. In a sense, each of the Book we create is also like a Directory highlighting contributing writers unique offerings. This has been a win-win for the contributing writers and authors.

Here is what our authors have said about working with us:

"I felt totally supported. The best bit was feeling like being part of a loving family who wants you to be your best, do your best, and is there for you every step of the way. It also boosted my confidence as a writer. The collaborative nature of the project also made it way more fun than doing things alone".
- Arrameia, Prague

"Visibility was a big piece of me coming out of the spiritual closet, and I felt that Radhaa Publishing House has a high energy and integrity level. Both of which are important for light workers and Starseeds. The curators and authors are light workers. Radhaa Publishing House created this wonderful opportunity for many others to be a part of. I felt that they put their whole heart into making this happen even before, during, and after the book is published. It was a project that was totally supportive that made me feel safe to share myself and my story." - Lalitah, Turkey

"It was wonderful to work with Radhaa Publishing House. I saw the effort and perseverance the whole team has and the support system they have for all the authors. I have matured as an author from this experience. I was so inspired after writing my chapter in this book, Awakening Starseeds, that I wrote an entire book called The Great Awakening because I was deeply moved writing."
- Leshara, Philippines

*"My story was edited by Radhaa Publishing House, and let me tell you, it put me in tears! They made it better than the way I originally wrote and submitted it while keeping my story and voice true to its events. I read it, and tears just flowed because it was so good!"- **Cristal, Florida***

*"I have published many books on Consciousness, empowerment subjects, and relationships, but I had never revealed raw, real stories of my life as with Awakening Starseeds. I wanted to join other authors writing personal stories, and Radhaa Publishing House made it simple and empowering to share from my heart in a real, raw way. This team of conscious, awesome Starseeds encourages a revolution to Awaken other Starseeds worldwide!" - **Stasia, Utah***

*This is an opportunity to STEP OUT, SPEAK OUR TRUTHS. This is our time, an obligation to share and support others that live in fear and question their soul paths, their soul journey. - **Breda, Canada***

At <u>**Radhaa Publishing House,**</u> we are highly involved in the entire process and work personally with the authors to navigate authorship challenges.

Our authors are heart-centered, soul-driven, and ready to manifest their legacy. We acknowledge the courage and strength it takes to step out into the public eye, and our team is here to support you all the way.

Creating a book is a tedious process and requires persistence, patience, and perspective. There are many moving parts of the book that need attention, and our team knows how to work hard to ensure we can come through with flying colors for the final date of our release.

Step into your voice and be heard now! When you become a contributing writer or an author of Radhaa Publishing House, you empower yourself in a way you may have never experienced before. That's what our authors tell us. Claim your author power now!

"Be that change you wanted to be in our world!"

If you have a compelling story to share with the world, dream of being a published author, and wish to be a part of the Radhaa Publishing family, reach out to us.

"No other publishing company offers you in-house support the way that Radhaa Publishing House does. Your legacy awaits!"

To find out more information about how to Join us,

Become an Author or See our Upcoming Books, please visit our Website at:

www.RadhaaPublishingHouse.com

Email: RadhaaPublishing@gmail.com

Thank you!

"You Make a Difference When You Support Our Holistic Books!"

Published Books:

Awakening Starseeds: Shattering Illusions, Vol.1

Awakening Starseeds: Stories Beyond The Stargate, Vol. 2

Quan Yin Goddess Activations™ Healing Workbook

Pillars of Light: Stories of Goddess Activations™

Energy Healing & Soul Medicine

Upcoming Books:

Awakening Starseeds: Dreaming into the Future, Vol. 3

Infinite Cosmic Records: Doorways to Healing

& Remembering

Memoirs of a Galactic Goddess Vol. 1

Memoirs of Galactic Goddess Vol. 2

Descendants of Lemuria

Where you can find Radhaa Publishing House Books:

Amazon.com — Barnes and Noble — Target

Walmart — Powell Books — Radhaa Publishing House

*Get your Signed Copy at Radhaa Publishing House

Online Store: https://radhaanilia.net/shop/

Email: RadhaaPublishing@gmail.com

Thank you for your support!

TO OUR READERS:

Dear Readers,

If you like our book, "Energy Healing & Soul Medicine," please support us by leaving a review.

REVIEW us ONLINE at: Amazon.com for *"ENERGY HEALING & SOUL MEDICINE"* book. We cannot do this without your support!

Share this journey with us. With Love & Gratitude, Thank you!

Energy Healing & Soul Medicine,
   Radhaa Nilia

RADHAA
PUBLISHING HOUSE

ENERGY
HEALING & SOUL
MEDICINE

Stories about Healing and Miracles
CURATED BY RADHAA NILIA

CPSIA information can be obtained
at www.ICGtesting.com
Printed in the USA
JSHW031119290522
26472JS00001B/62